GREEN IS NOT A COLOR!

A PROFESSIONAL CHRONICLE TO INTERIOR DESIGN SUCCESS

JULIE REGAN SMITH

Green Emerald Press—Carefree, AZ
ISBN: 979-8-218-16124-8
Library of Congress Control Number: 2023904611
Title: *Green Is Not A Color! A Professional Chronicle to Interior Design Success*
Author: Julie Regan Smith
Digital distribution | 2023
Paperback | 2023

DEDICATION

This book is dedicated with much gratitude to the following:

To my best friend and husband Greg, who totally gets me. His love, support, patience, encouragement, and guidance in my journey of writing down my experiences in order to create, write and complete this book is worthy of Olympic Gold. No one makes me laugh like you do!

To my amazing children Bobby and Madi, who continue to delight me with their insightfulness, strength, success, and kindness, I am so very proud.

To those dear clients, who inspired this book and will not read it…bless them!

Disclaimer: Most of what follows is true. The names are made up and any resemblance to persons living or deceased should be plainly apparent to them and those who know them.

TABLE OF CONTENTS

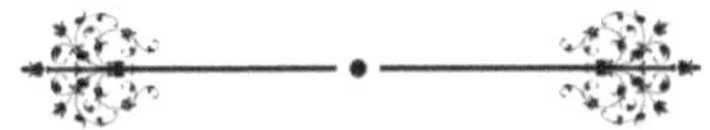

INTRODUCTION
GREEN IS NOT A COLOR – HOW IT ALL STARTED

According to Elizabeth, a former client of mine, green is *not* a color. Elizabeth declared this as we were getting to know each other while skimming through fabric swatches, a task we had been arduously working on for four hours straight. Of course, at the time I thought what a fascinating statement, not only preposterous, but also not accurate. I could not resist asking her what on Earth she meant. Well according to Elizabeth,

"The reason green is not a color is because it's everywhere."

"Okay, I'll bite," I said. After all, I couldn't let this opportunity slip by.

So, I asked her, "Would you care to explain or expand on this notion of yours?"

Elizabeth continued to explain to me that trees, grass, and plants are all green. Therefore, green is not a color. "And besides," she added, "…green goes with everything!"

'Well,' I thought to myself, '…potatoes pretty much go with everything, so does that exempt them from being a vegetable?'

These days, many things in life shock me, but I think this is the first time in my career I was truly mystified by one of my clients. Elizabeth's notion was completely off the wall. I had to resist all temptation to challenge her. But I held my tongue because; well, because I really wanted her as a client. On top of that, I wanted to further explore what led her to such a sacrilegious (well, in the design world) observation. Where did this theory of hers come from? My mind was reeling, goading me to debate Elizabeth further. Say it, my mind demanded; say "Green is in fact a color!" If you mix the primary colors, yellow and blue together, *surprise!* You get the secondary color known universally as green, grün, vert, viridis, and groente. Whatever, I'm not picky, just call it what it is.

Looking back, my interaction with Elizabeth was a red flag – pigment pun intended – which I later wished I hadn't ignored. She grew to be one of the most difficult clients I had ever worked with. Although everything turned out well in the end, it took a lot of hard work on my part to try and please 'No-Go Green' Elizabeth.

Ah, but this is just one of the many great things about interior design, each project was as unique as the individual, which made it exciting, challenging, interesting and at times bewildering. I never grew weary of immersing myself in the research and fast pace the industry demanded of me. Finding the perfect fabrics, textures, furniture, light fixtures, or whatever the project required, always taught me something new.

MY HISTORY – YAWN…

I have always been fascinated and intrigued by history. Not *my* history necessarily, but history in general. Let me explain. Initially I planned to take on archeology as a career. The thought of discovering artifacts hundreds or even thousands of years old captivated me beyond belief. I had the opportunity during my early college years to go on an archeological dig. That single experience taught me more than I ever knew about myself. I won't bore you with all the fine details, just know I came to the realization that archeologists are always covered in dirt, and they never get to wear great shoes. Need I say more?

Yup, one dig and I was done. I was on to my next college experience as a double major in Art and Psychology. I have always loved children and art also had a special place in my heart. This double major would allow me to have my cake and eat it too. Meaning I could use art to help children. Well, after a few semesters I had quickly realized this was not my path. There was one tiny problem with working alongside children in the mental health field – I wanted to take every single one of those precious kids home with me and care for them. Not quite a viable plan.

Thus, I made an appointment with my college counselor. She suggested various paths for me to research; computer sciences, (yawn); biology, (…me, in a lab coat? No thanks); culinary arts (I can barely make ice); and theater (self-explanatory). You get the point; the list goes on and on. Although these are all noteworthy majors anyone should be proud of, they just didn't spark anything in me.

Finally, when I was on my counselor's last nerve, which by the way she had no intention of hiding, she mentioned the field of Interior Design. The problem was, in the mid-1970's there were very few schools offering an Interior Design program. In fact, Interior

Design was often shoved against its will under the umbrella of the Department of Home Economics. Ah yes, would you like a dozen fresh baked cookies with your new sleeper sofa? Hello, we're not baking cookies here! Don't get me wrong, there's nothing wrong with baking, or cookies. But Home Economics? Really? Anyway, I finally found and graduated from a university in Los Angeles with a Bachelor of Science degree in Interior Design and a minor in Business. The ideal marriage for what was to come.

Although I was having the time of my life with my classmates, I vividly remember a moment the night we graduated when one of my professors looked directly at me and said with a smirk, "Now you're ready for a real education." No truer words were spoken. And what makes it true is that there are so many moving parts to being an interior designer. *None* of which I was taught in school. Sound familiar? My *real* education started when I was offered a full-time position working for one of the best interior designers in LA. This is where I really learned my craft, made real mistakes which usually cost me real money, real time, and big-time real embarrassment. All hard lessons learned, mostly the hard way. On a positive note, remember that Psychology major I dabbled in? I will say it served me well in working with some of these LA bred clients.

I honed my trade over 30 years in both commercial and residential design. Before I knew it, I earned the title of interior designer. I felt and still feel that there is a significant difference between an interior designer and an interior decorator. I found throughout my career that many people called themselves 'interior designers' – but they were not. Sure sometimes I have a headache and with one click of the internet I can self-diagnose, but does this make me a doctor? If it does, we're all doomed. In fact, to this day, if someone calls me an interior 'decorator' it makes me bristle. I still feel compelled to kindly explain the difference between an interior designer and an interior decorator.

I believe an interior decorator looks at a space and sees a room they can aesthetically furnish and accessorize. They wonder how they can adequately fill the room with complementary colors and the appropriate size sofa. An interior designer looks at a space and envisions a blank canvas. They take in the environment, the character, and most importantly, the occupants. They note the size of the entire space, the year it was built, and if it will serve a family of five or a bachelor. Will it be a great room for lavish gatherings that will showcase fine art and silk window treatments? Or will it be a cozy den with soft lighting for little ones to watch movies and build forts? My point is an interior designer looks at the macro-space and its endless possibilities.

Additionally, a professional interior designer holds a degree from an accredited college. It's a four-year degree and in some universities, it takes a full five years to complete. Personally, I do not believe a two-year degree or certificate is adequate. As a side note, my colleagues tell me that an interior designer will have to be licensed in the not-so-distant future, and rightly so.

I would consider myself remiss if I failed to mention those I worked alongside throughout my career. During my years in the interior design business the office personnel, my colleagues, junior design assistants, and vendors were very much an indispensable part of my success. There were often many moving parts to the projects I undertook, each part interwoven with the team. They certainly contributed and aided in my accomplishments by giving me the tools to be awarded and successfully complete a project. Even as good as I thought I was, I could not have done it all without the support of a great team.

What follows is a collection of thoughts, impressions, and adventures mixed with solid industry standard advice about what I experienced and applied as an interior designer. It basically spans the last decade of my work in the design field.

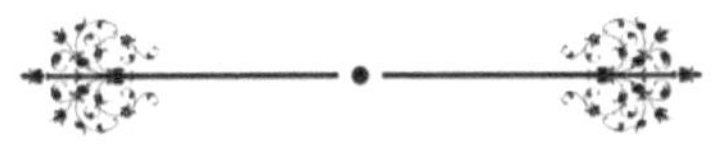

PROLOGUE
WHY WRITE A BOOK ABOUT MY CAREER?

To put it simply – I loved my career and wanted to share my experiences, passion, pain, and growth with anyone who cared to listen. This insight led me to ask a variety of questions. What pearls of wisdom could I pass along? What did my career teach me? Why did I choose interior design in the first place? Most importantly perhaps is, why am I choosing to go through the process of writing this if the outcome might be nothing? This last question is the easiest to answer – I strongly believe that we need to do the things that make us happy, and writing this book truly made me happy.

When I began to reflect and respond to these and other questions, I thought to myself, did I really think that about my client? Did I really create something so beautiful? Did I really just say that out loud? This in turn led me to think to myself, I wonder if anyone else might find what I've learned interesting, or dare I say even helpful? Well, there is only one way to find out – that's when I began writing. And apparently, I had a lot to say.

When I was tasked with a design project I was encouraged to utilize and develop my creative skills to the best of my abilities. So, I boldly forged ahead with the notion that the sky's the limit, and I was going to take full advantage of that limit. This allowed me to set my artistry free which, essentially, allowed it the power to flourish and have a life of its own. This attitude was truly a gift I was given, and it set the stage for the skills I obtained along the way, none of which I will ever take for granted. In return, I felt it was my duty to share the rare blessings and frequent hardships I discovered that brought me such gratitude – in hopes it may do the same for you.

Regarding hardships, there were many – and I mean many times I had to work with clients in let's call them "difficult" situations. I taught myself to take the high road and not take these interactions so seriously. Sometimes I felt this was a difficult pill to swallow, but over time I learned that it was a lesson worth the discomfort. What good does it do to be angry, impatient, and resentful anyway? This only created negative energy that I quickly learned was not constructive for anyone.

I know, I know. People always say if they had to do it all over again, they wouldn't change a thing. Well, I am here to say I am no different than those said people. I had victories that were oh-so-sweet which acted as my little soldiers that stood behind me in battle and encouraged me to conquer my fears. But make no mistake, there were also enemies that were able to cross the battlefield and break through my stronghold resulting in my defeat. Even though there were successes and failures, it molded me into the woman, mother, and person I am today.

My career offered me many golden opportunities and I grabbed as many of those opportunities I could as they came. I often had to ask myself, 'Am I willing to do the heavy lifting or not?' No, not just lifting heavy furniture – tee hee – I mean, am I willing to do the work, gain experience and be all that I can be? Well you're damn right I can, and I am here to say, so can you!

Allow me to offer a word of advice before we move ahead. Whatever you do and wherever life takes you, don't forget to nurture the child that is still within us all. Let the giggles slip out and smile for cryin' out loud! See the positive side of everyone and everything. Yes, I know this can be hard work and tedious at times. But make it a habit. And remember, do what you love and love what you do. Be your authentic self because that is the person you will love and want to know.

Author, Elizabeth Gilbert, conveniently and affably sums up best why I wrote this book, *"... at the end of your creative adventure, you have a souvenir – something that you made, something to remind you forever of your brief but transformative encounter with inspiration."*

MY PICTURE VS. A THOUSAND WORD QUANDARY

Is a picture really worth a thousand words? Depends on the picture I suppose. I wrestled with the option of including pictures of my work with the hope it would speak a thousand words. Turns out, I found more enjoyment writing about what those pictures represented than I did pouring over photographs of possible entries. So, after serious thought I decided, I'm not going to make a glossy hardback photo book that will inevitably find its way to a dusty resting place cluttering someone's cocktail table. In fact, I would much rather find it standing at the ready, dusty or not, in someone's office bookcase.

Another thing, like fashion, art, architecture, nutrition, and music, the turnover of popular interior design trends generally only last two or three years. In the design world, it often started with a color craze that usually trended for about a year at most. What is today's latest trend in the design world can transform overnight. This led me to the conviction that if I tattooed the pages of this book with lavish glossy photos of my work it would merely 'date stamp' my work and ultimately overshadow what I hope to convey in my writing.

Finally, there's a practical reason for omitting photos. It's expensive, and for God's sake, I'm not Martha Stewart. Besides, this is my first attempt at writing – yes, you read that correctly please try and contain your shock.

CHAPTER 1
IT'S BUSINESS, NOT PERSONAL

I first heard this line in a movie, and although it's considered a business axiom, I must respectfully disagree. In the world of interior design, it's both business *and* personal. While you are with your clients mulling over cabinet colors and area rugs for hours on end, you may – sorry, you *will* – walk into your office one day, sit down with a hot vanilla latté so graciously delivered to you by said client, and find yourself completely and utterly embedded in their personal lives.

Let me explain. As an interior designer, it goes without saying I obviously had to be inside their homes, but I also had to be inside their heads. What I mean by this is it's especially important to be aware of how they interacted with their spouses, partners, significant other, children, and even their pets. I found it helpful to understand the dynamics of these relationships. Doing so helped me better understand how to design a project.

I made it my mission to learn how they lived day to day. I pictured and studied their face when something caught their eye, made note of every little comment they murmured. My brain was always bursting at the seams with files full of information on how they lounged, how they relaxed, how they entertained, how they cleaned, how they slept, and curiously, what they noticed when they visited a friend's home. In other words, what speaks to them not only in comfort, form, and function, but color, textures, and lighting as well.

It is also important to understand the client's feeling of pride and ownership. Being skilled in recognizing and anticipating your client's needs, dreams and desires is essential to not only having a successful client relationship but getting it right for them – the first time. As their interior designer you must remember, it's always about 'them,' not you. Clients are the main character, and you are the supporting actor. Your number one priority is to do everything possible to make them feel like a star and help them deliver a blockbuster film.

For the last six years of my career, I worked in a boutique showroom that offered considerable flexibility of services. The showroom could deliver all the client's needs whether it be Computer-Aided Design (CAD), furniture, finishes, flooring, window treatments, lighting, or remodeling.

The showroom's flexibility made it easy for clients to pick and choose from what I liked to call the 'menu.' Featured on the menu was a variety of vignettes showcasing different interior design styles, from contemporary to traditional, southwest to coastal, minimalism to Hollywood glam, and so on. Clients could conveniently explore the showroom's menu items, weigh their options, and see what they liked or disliked. I found that it made clients a bit more comfortable when they were empowered by menu choices.

The showroom was also a very useful place to make a client's experience personal and safe. By safe I mean the showroom acted as a haven where clients could confidently (and sometimes confidentially) express their thoughts and ideas without judgment. I always encouraged those who visited the showroom to unwind, chat about their ideas, show me pictures of what they had in mind, enlighten me about their wishes, and while we're at it perhaps have a glass of wine. Many times, it was their input about what they saw in the showroom that spurred some of my best ideas and inspirations.

Don't forget that everyone has a story. But sometimes clients have a difficult time expressing what they truly want, what they actually need and if they really understand what it takes to accomplish their dream…their story. Sometimes their story involved past experiences with a home, a contractor, or a designer that regrettably did not end well. Maybe they are choosing to downsize to a smaller home or outfitting a new second home. Sometimes their story was about changing lifestyles, perhaps they just retired, recently became empty nesters, now have grandchildren, or they are just plain tired of the current style they have been living with for so long and are ready for a change. My point is, you never create the same end result twice, and to tell you a secret... that's the best part of interior design.

Understanding their story gave me the tools to do my job. When I discover their main 'storyline,' I can accomplish the task at hand and begin to further develop their narrative. After all, as their interior designer I wanted to help them turn the page to a new chapter in their lives and assist them in navigating their way through the challenges of transforming their ideas into reality. I considered myself the co-author of their story – I researched, edited, verified, and supported. As an interior designer, you will come to wear many hats.

As I said, I always told clients that their project is about them and not me. A lot of clients found this concept peculiar. The reason being is many clients have worked with interior designers who are bound to their own trademark style. This often resulted in clients feeling obliged to honor the trademark instead of following their own wishes. I assured clients that this was their home, their style, and their life, and if they don't love it in the showroom, they definitely won't love it in their home. Besides, I did not want all my projects to be basic, cookie-cutter rehashes of some sort of trademark. Instead, I told them I wanted a challenge.

A challenge to me is a husband and wife walking into the showroom and expressing completely opposite styles, a businesswoman telling me she has three kids and two dogs but loves the color white, and a young man pointing out the most expensive pieces of art we have on the wall then proceeds to tell me about his strict budget. I wanted to devise a plan so cohesive, so inclusive, and so brilliant that even the pickiest of clients would walk into their home and be in awe. The goal of the challenge is for them to walk into their home, love what they see, smile and be happy! Simple concept! I wanted to do the research and create a project that excited my clients, and I wanted a project that got me excited as well.

By the way, clients are much more creative than they often think. They gave me hints, glimpses, and ideas of what they like, and certainly what they did not like. For example, they like reds and yellows, but hated orange. They tell me they like contemporary but not modern. A client's creativity notwithstanding, I occasionally found they rarely understood the sometimes-subtle differences in styles. But that did not matter. There's no need to label a style in my opinion. I believed it was my job to blend different designs with the goal of defining my client's own unique, personal style.

If a client was hell-bent to define a style I would simply tell them, '...the style will be between traditional and contemporary.' Okay, I know what you are thinking. That's a rather broad spectrum of styles that pretty much covers everything from the Stone Age to what is trending this very moment. But on many occasions, I had clients get unnecessarily frustrated in trying to define and label the style they were trying to achieve. If they stated the look they were going for I would walk them through the showroom and point out examples of that style. Utilizing furnishings in the showroom as a model helped me to define what the clients were after. Besides, it was rare to find a client that loved every single aspect of one specific interior design style.

When in doubt I would suggest a 'soft contemporary' or 'transitional' style to avoid extremes. Above all, I recommended they purchase what they love. I reminded them that even though they were pining for a mid-century modern look, they didn't have to buy the low sitting, teal velvet sofa that they honestly didn't really like. This approach seemed to work, and it was also less intimidating for clients. Doing so often allowed us to break a creative log jam and move forward. Clients had a sense of relief about this, and so did I.

FIRST CONTACT

The showroom I worked in was in a high traffic retail shopping center. People were constantly stopping in to browse or admire the vast selection of the showroom's high-end furnishings. Approaching a stranger and making contact is always a bit awkward, but I found that being myself and being respectful went a long way when speaking with prospective clients. I think I developed an instinct, and you will too, to sense when it's the appropriate time to approach someone and start a conversation. Believe me; you will know immediately if they are not receptive. But having the ability to make a friend in sixty-seconds was a little technique I perfected over time. It's quite a simple technique really, just smile, find something in common such as clothing, where they're from, whether they are new to the area and then, listen. Oh, and one other thing, eye contact goes a long way.

I believe I attracted clients by how I presented myself with personal style, manners, and how I looked. I know that we don't like to admit it but at some point, or another, we all find ourselves judging a book by its cover. I always felt I was being judged when first speaking with a client – judged by my looks, judged by my demeanor, and judged by my personality.

One day, a very good client commented on what I was wearing and said, "You always look so beautiful."

When I thanked her, she said, "I have found the best interior designers I have worked with over the years, know how to dress."

There you have it. Dress the part and show off your personal style. After all, Tom Ford said it best, "...*dressing well is a form of good manners*."

Not to sound all "six-degrees of separation" about it but I believe there is usually a thread of commonality I was able to draw out little by little that eventually unraveled a client's story. So, when I approached a client for the first time, I'd keep in mind that we are all connected. Once I discovered a commonality, people would begin to unfold. In my opinion, being open, sincere, and interested in someone as a person and not just a client is the first step to making them feel comfortable.

I was always mindful to be patient with clients, not to rush or distract from the 'something' a client may be about to reveal. By discovering this 'something,' I could begin to build a relationship. I know it sounds like a very small step, but it worked for me. No one wants to be hounded when shopping. A no pressure conversation usually put a smile on their face.

With experience also came the sense to recognize when someone was not interested. In those cases, I would simply invite them to browse, explore the showroom, and let them know if they had questions, I would be happy to assist. I politely handed them my business card which effectively put them in control.

Naturally, my goal was to have the client make an appointment with me before they left the showroom. However, this was not always an easy goal to achieve. I often strategized by asking myself what I could do to keep them from leaving the showroom without concocting some ridiculous delay tactic, or, you know – kidnapping them. Since I only had seconds before a client walked away, I had to think at warp speed whether I had overlooked a clue to keeping them interested. Or maybe I missed an opening to boldly invite myself to their home? I thought, 'How can I lasso them with my ever-so-appealing personality?'

Anyhow, in the beginning I was constantly second guessing myself, a habit I had to drop and ultimately did – a totally exhausting but necessary process by the way. I realized that sometimes I simply needed to self-examine and adjust my approach.

I always convinced clients it was important for me to come to their home. So, setting an appointment was essential. I explained that visiting their home helped me define those pieces, such as sentimental artwork or invaluable 'sacred' family heirlooms that would remain integral to the overall design. During the home visit I would explore their likes and dislikes, what they wanted to change, and the overall end goal for their space. In other words, get to know them and the world they hope to one day live in.

One of the most exciting things for me was inviting clients to my office where I pulled up my calendar, have them give me their personal information and schedule an on-site appointment. At this point I felt I had won them over, just a little, and we were on our way to a new adventure – together. It was at this moment I found it difficult to contain myself. My excitement and enthusiasm were genuine, which was often contagious for clients.

It was always encouraging after I had persuaded clients to commit to an in-home consultation. It was confirmation that I had approached them correctly, we began to connect, and they had become comfortable enough to invite me into their home. After all, a person's home is an extremely personal and vulnerable space, and I felt nothing short of honored when they welcomed me into that world of theirs. Making the first in-home appointment I felt like we were building not just a business relationship, but more of a business *friendship*. And as their friend, I assured them I would be by their side and have their back. I was in no way there to judge them as a homeowner. I was there first and foremost to get a glimpse into their world.

BABY STEPS

During the first onsite visit I requested a tour of the entire home even if I am only designing one room. It helps me get the lay of the land, so to speak. Because I was an invited guest, my experience taught me to take baby steps.

The first baby-step – listen! I want the clients to run the show in their own home. As I said, I am a guest and I wanted plenty of opportunity to listen, observe, learn, and absorb as much as I could about their lives and home or at least as much as they wanted to share with me. I often asked clients, "How do you see yourself living in this space?"

Any input I received would assist me in the project. Always – and this pairs nicely with the listening step – write down everything you can that you see or hear. Since this is our first meeting, and we are still getting to know each other I don't want clients to feel pressured. I strived to help them relax, by chatting casually while I gently navigate the discussion. But listening is, in my opinion, the very first baby-step of successful salesmanship. You can have all the artistic talent in the world, but if you can't listen – you can't, and won't, sell.

The second and more practical baby-step is – take measurements. Once a client is on-board, take measurements of the project space that will be used to create floor plans. Also, take pictures of everything so you can easily look back and jog your memory. After taking measurements and pictures, it is especially important to, jot down your client's needs, thoughts, problems, concerns and whatever else they may want to throw at you. By taking notes, it really shows the client you are listening to what they want and that you are genuinely interested and focused. While building a foundation for their project you can really see how people live and feel about their home, about themselves, their partners, and so on. By absorbing and storing this information I often began to develop a pathway that guided me to see specific design possibilities.

The third baby-step is – evaluate. I was often asked to work with existing flooring, furniture, art, lighting, and so on. Use all the skills, tips, tricks, and strategies you will learn, to understand what can stay, what must go, and what needs to change.

THE BLESSING OF 'SACRED' ITEMS

I define what I call 'sacred' items as family heirlooms or anything in a client's home that must remain or is deemed non-negotiable. I felt the baby steps described above were necessary to navigate the decision-making process when clients wanted to retain 'sacred' items. As their interior designer I first understood how blessed sacred items were to clients and then considered how to make them work. How will these artifacts make design sense, and ultimately compliment and contribute to the overall style we are after? This often required me to pull a rabbit out of a hat, which I couldn't always do, but was sure as hell willing to try. Allow me to share a few anecdotes related to 'sacred' items.

ICKY WICKER

Louise was a cranky, 'Get off my lawn!' kind of lady who wanted me to modernize her furnishings before she placed her home on the market. Before I even rang the doorbell, Louise was standing at the ready to welcome my crew and I…, sort of. She stood firmly planted, centered in the doorway in her thin floral dress which seemed to be glued to her petite frame. Louise's wrinkled face was as stern and scolding as my eighth-grade parochial schoolteacher, Sister Benedict. Louise's gaze was clearly fixed on my assistant who was immediately told, not *asked* mind you, to remove his shoes. Next, she eyed my ever-stylish footwear, and I was granted entry without reprimand. Apparently, I was allowed to keep my shoes on. Hurray for designer footwear! A small victory indeed – which I greatly appreciated.

Upon entering the great-room, I was greeted with a very tidy, clean, and well cared for abode, except for one glaring detail. Louise had white painted wicker furniture that was in such ill repair and so parched that it looked as though it had spent weeks, no, *months* in the direct afternoon sun of the Sahara Desert. Each piece was seriously on the verge of becoming dust and was indiscriminately scattered throughout her home. Her icky wicker was mixed in with other beautiful pieces of furniture without any thought or intention of how it fit or looked for that matter. Talk about a full-fledged eye assault. Time for a bonfire, I thought. Anyone got a light?

My mission, if I chose to accept it, was to update her home to be more comfortable, modern, inviting, and marketable. The problem though was Louise was delighted with her icky wicker.

"The wicker stays," she stated. "I've had those pieces for a long time."

'You don't say,' I thought. Should I just tell her the Bedouin people just called and asked for their furniture back?

We continued our tour and noticed she had a couple of half empty bedrooms. 'Hmm… now here's a possibility,' I thought. We finished our tour at which point Louise and I chatted about what she ultimately wanted. I suggested that to achieve her goals we needed to relocate all, and I mean *all* the wicker furniture.

"Here's what you can do with it," I told her, "Place it in one of the half empty bedrooms." (Sometimes you have to tell the client what they didn't know they needed to hear.)

I explained to her that this will create a brand-new room that could be a place of repose for her. Ah-ha! See what I did there?

Louise was thrilled and thoroughly embraced the idea. Approaching the conditions of her project this way accomplished not only getting the contract but did so without any bruised feelings. We cobbled together a design plan that included those things she was obviously attached to and created a place of serenity. The result…one special room for one special lady! With the quick fix of relocating the icky wicker complete I could concentrate on transforming the main rooms of her home.

Being gentle, gracious, and respectful with clients without telling them their 'sacred' items were sometimes more cursed than sacred took finesse. Applying this finesse comes with experience and awareness. After time you'll gain the savvy to manage these types of situations which, in the end, always seem to work out in the best way. On to the next sacred item challenge.

Aunt Mildred's Monstrosity

Janet had a chandelier smack-dab in the middle of her dining room. It was an inheritance from her Aunt Mildred, but the piece could only be described as a monstrosity. The first thing I thought when I saw it was, did Aunt Mildred have a vendetta? A chandelier this special should be in a place where it can truly shine, think run-down casino or a smoke-filled pool hall. Okay, I'll stop being mean, it's not like I said any of this out loud.

So, my discussion with Janet went something like this;

"Janet, we need to consider a few things here. Considering the size of your room, and the size and style of your dining table and chairs, and last but certainly not least, the size and look of your chandelier just does not work."

Janet confessed she felt the chandelier was not the best fit. Especially if she wanted to achieve the refreshing modern look she longed for. To say I was relieved she saw it the same way as I, was an understatement. But I needed a solution. I thought back to when I was greeted at Janet's front door and invited in, I remembered thinking that she had a very large entry with a very tall ceiling. Ta-Dah! Why not place the chandelier there? It would certainly be an object of interest and it would be an appropriate fit for the space. She agreed and I knew immediately I could forge ahead with the rest of her project without Aunt Mildred's monstrosity looming overhead.

There's A Canoe In The Zoo

And finally – Fred. What a sporty kind of guy he was! The entrance to his very large home was laden with sacred goodies. One of which was a canoe. Yes, a canoe. The paddle-powered craft you generally place in the water – but not in your home.

Fred led the way into his ginormous two-story den that displayed a vast variety of taxidermy game trophies he had installed. Motionless beasts, birds, and reptiles with unwavering dead eyes watched every corner of the room. Although an impressive collection, Fred's den could scare the daylights out of anyone, even Steven King. It seemed as though at any moment one of these creatures could come alive, jump off the wall and tear you to pieces. The den's walls were enhanced with landscaped creations arranged with mounds of faux rocks, grass, and trees which were all mounted beneath a bright blue cloudless sky painted on the ceiling. The lighting was engineered to brilliantly highlight each creature. The centerpiece of Fred's home was a veritable museum of Natural History.

This place could easily be a setting for a Hitchcock movie, I thought. I have to admit though, I did find it intriguing. Fred stood in the middle of the room beaming with pride over his favorite room in the home… his beloved den. As an interior designer, how could I not appreciate this kind of dedication to one's personal style? Fred was obviously a world traveler who clearly had a lot of interesting stories to tell.

After several moments of surveying the room, and trying not to gawk while taking in this still life zoo, I said, "So Fred, you told me you just needed a new office desk chair as I recall, right?"

"Yes, and a few other items as well," he said. "But first, I would like your thoughts on placing my canoe."

I knew there was no talking Fred out of his canoe (pun intended). He insisted on keeping it inside because he had had so many adventures in the now sacred vessel.

I had to think fast, so after bouncing a few ideas around in my head, I came up with a few suggestions.

Since the canoe was retired, one option I offered was perhaps stand the canoe upright with its oars, or paddles, or whatever the heck you propel a canoe with. I thought, to accommodate the canoe, he just needs to make a few small adjustments to one or two stuffed vermin. Another idea I had was to hang it on the wall and place some of his treasured memorabilia in the canoe and make it a sort of display piece, or at the very least something a bit more functional.

One final suggestion was to artfully hang the canoe from the ceiling – if you can call a hanging canoe art. To do this a few adjustments needed to be made, but nothing major. Happily, Fred liked the ideas and stated he needed time to think about his options. He told me he appreciated my suggestions and asked if I would assist in the final placement. How could I pass up this offer?

"Of course I will," I said. I also wanted to tell him that I would wear my best camo. Fred ultimately went with the option to 'artistically' hang the canoe from the ceiling.

I had many types of design challenges that were governed by a sacred item. I always found it fascinating that clients who claimed ownership to the unusual were often just as interesting and unusual as the items they kept. As their interior designer, they did me a great service by reminding me to always keep an open mind, be courteous and non-judgmental, and most of all remain calm and carry on. I learned that these were key components when working with clients that were just, shall we say, a little more eccentric. Their treasures were very personal, and I'll say sacred to them in their own right. If their treasures were personal and emotional enough to be the object in which they designed their entire home around, they earned the right to be called sacred.

THE FIRST DATE

If all went well during our first in-home visit, I scheduled what I coined the 'first date.' The first date was a design presentation in the showroom. Just like any first date, it can be a little nerve racking. What should I say? What should I wear? Will they like me? And as their potential interior designer, will they love what I am presenting?

Preparation for the first date began with very high expectations. I was always editing and perfecting the presentation right up until the last moment. I knew clients were excited about the presentation, but I also knew they wanted to be impressed. I uploaded site visit photos of a client's home to my computer and reviewed them multiple times keeping in mind various avenues and options I could present. I memorized details about every room so I could speak comfortably and confidently about possible changes and updates we could explore together. I did my homework and was ready to make recommendations with ease. The point of all my diligence was to demonstrate early on that there was no doubt I wanted the project, that I could complete the project, and that I know how to make that happen.

My goal during the first date is to win their trust and prove to them that I am worthy of their business and assure them I am a professional. This is where I would mention my education and experience in design and reiterate that I have the skills needed to make their dreams become reality and all within a budget.

CHAPTER 2
PRESENTATIONS – IT'S SHOW TIME!

Setting up a presentation always excited me. It was a time I relished because it felt like being on stage. To be frank, I enjoyed being in the spotlight and doing presentations. I found myself becoming quite animated about my projects because I always worked extremely hard to create a masterful presentation. It was the time I could really demonstrate that I was a professional, prepared and committed. I wanted clients to see my passion and how driven I was when it came to my craft.

By the way, getting clients involved and participating in the presentation helps everyone relax. Doing so gave me another opportunity to observe their personalities, how they interacted, and how *we* interacted. My one goal at this point was to make the presentation as beautiful, concise, and effortless as possible. Building trust is also a very big part of a presentation and should not be overlooked or taken for granted. You can easily build trust by including certain details clients mentioned during the home visit. In my experience, when I first began a design presentation, it was all adrenaline, which faded into butterflies and then – pure excitement.

It is also important to mention I strived to make the presentation fun from start to finish. After all, clients were very likely going to be spending hard-earned money and they wanted it to be meticulous – and rightfully so. As the interior designer and self-appointed director, so to speak, making sure my presentations were fun, exciting and entertaining (which they were) established a sense of confidence in my abilities.

When preparing for a presentation, I always reserved back-up design options just in case. I organized my presentations in layers and strived to inspire visuals for clients. The first layer was the home's existing floor plan or, in the case of a remodel, the proposed floor plan. Flooring, furnishings, fabrics, finishes, light fixtures, and lastly, window treatments were the other layers. I preferred to create at least three different design schemes for each layer.

When I pulled products for a presentation, I included a tear sheet with pricing for my project bin. A project bin, by the way, is where I gathered samples, plans, pictures, and tear sheets that had all the information I needed to specify and order product. Tear sheets are important because they detailed product prices, manufacturers, item numbers and descriptions. By accessing and referring to various manufacturers' websites I was able to see if a specific item was in stock or backordered.

Having informational tear sheets at my fingertips was also important because if there happened to be a time crunch on a project, and the lead time was excessively delayed on a manufacturer's product; I would eliminate it from the presentation. It is an incredibly bad feeling when a client falls in love with a piece of furniture, and I have to tell them it won't be available for 18 months or possibly more. Of course, there were always exceptions to eliminating items from a presentation, especially if the product I had chosen was an absolute showstopper to the client.

Tear sheets also provided me with the power to calculate percentage mark ups making it easy for me to accurately calculate project costs for clients. When selections were finalized, I was able to use the tear sheet to take stock of the potentially hundreds of moving parts involved in a project, which also lessened the margin of error. As you can see, a tear sheet is an essential element of a presentation.

As I became more experienced in presenting, I noticed that people were very visual and simply seeing the eye-candy I presented usually got clients on-board right then and there. Now, what I am about to say next may sound counterintuitive, but I felt I did my job when clients had a tough time making their selections. What I mean is, it implied that they loved everything, and it was a challenge for them to finalize their selections. Like I said about the three design options, it's better to have too many options, than not enough.

Here's a tip - it's wise to include a few oddball items in a presentation that are clearly outside the design palette (especially when dealing with more 'difficult' clients). Doing so offers clients something to say no to. Yes, I know this sounds manipulative, but there is a method to my madness. Having more than less allows for wiggle-room when it comes down to making final choices. Do not underestimate this tip because I promise, it is a powerful one. Providing clients the option to say no to certain items or choose a different route is a great way of enticing them into the project.

It empowers them to take ownership. Although some clients will require the interior designer to do it all, most really do enjoy participating in the design process.

MY D.A. IS BETTER THAN YOUR D.A.

I considered myself very fortunate to have an interior design assistant (D.A.) with me during my presentations. My assistant helped by researching furniture pieces, case goods (any furniture that is not upholstered), finishes, light fixtures, and at times edited drawings as well. By drawings I mean CAD (Computer Aided Drawings). There were many times when I needed additional furniture options, plans edited, or elevations of a space that would make clear what I wanted to convey. Having an assistant who understood the project and understood how I worked was huge for me. They were able to pull fabrics and finishes before, or during a presentation which saved valuable time. D.A.s can be an essential part of making a presentation cohesive.

There is a definite art to choosing and presenting the four Fs – furniture, fabrics, fixtures, and finishes. This is where having a qualified assistant is vital when compiling the four Fs for multiple projects. Personally, I define a solid interior design assistant by their familiarity with the project at hand, knowledge of the showroom's manufacturers, a sense of urgency, and the ability to read my mind (kidding of course). On a serious note, it is very important to establish a connection with your team – this will show during a presentation. For example, if a D.A. is able to pull an item that needs to be modified during a presentation, the D.A. can quickly retrieve alternate 'F's (furniture, fabric, fixtures and finishes in case you forgot) on the fly. Meanwhile, the lead interior designer can continue with the presentation.

THE $$$ TABLE

During my showroom presentations I preferred using a long, wide counter height table. I light-heartedly referred to this table as the *money table*. This was where it all came together; the furnishings estimate, the deposit, and the signed contract. The convenience of the money table allowed clients to touch samples, ponder their options, and rearrange to their liking until they had a clear picture of everything I had laid out. Interaction at the money table made clients feel like they were part of the presentation. Remember, as thrilling as it is for you, it's still about 'them.'

NOT IN THE MOOD SWINGS

Another skill that I developed is to be able to recognize and change direction of a presentation on the fly. Clients can potentially become overwhelmed during a presentation. Perhaps I was speaking too fast, maybe I didn't fully explain the direction I was headed, or maybe I just didn't get it right this time. That's when it's time to pause and get them back in the game. This can be done by simply asking, "Tell me what you like or dislike."

I have found clients appreciated being asked and were often willing to allow time to take a break, regroup, or simply walk the showroom and explore other options. Sometimes I would stop and say that our project is still evolving – meaning we do not have to decide right now and could shelve the issue for the moment. We could easily come back to whatever seemed to be the stumbling block so I could keep the presentation moving forward. I was always mindful of being prepared to switch gears and adjust to what clients told me. Doing so gave me the opportunity to right the ship.

On another note, the presentation process should not be rushed. I made sure I had scheduled plenty of time to spend with clients. There were always adjustments made during the presentation process and I never wanted to show tension, annoyance, or have them feel hurried. Sometimes, clients loved most of the design but maybe wanted to see more of a certain color (like green perhaps), or a different chair, or they simply needed a break.

If, however, the presentation went smoothly, everything was finalized with a client and the cost estimate was reviewed. I was also very clear about communicating product delivery dates, installation, and construction progress if a remodel was part of a project. Before clients pulled the trigger and decided to go ahead with a project, I was sure to tell them that once items are ordered I did not always have control over when they would be received. There is always the chance there could be supply-chain issues, delayed turnaround times, or backordered materials. These types of delays always had a bearing on when a project could be installed. Sure, products may be in stock today, but by the time we sent the order to the manufacturer, and by the time the manufacturer sends back an acknowledgement, it's possible they may not have enough material to complete the order.

This can happen especially when ordering a sample for approval. Meaning, the interior designer has requested a finished wood or metal sample or wants to make sure a fabric's dye lot (color and pattern) is a correct match. The process of requesting a sample goes something like this; the manufacturer receives the sample request, the manufacturer sends the requested sample, the interior designer receives the sample, then the interior designer (and sometimes the client) approves or disapproves the sample. This process obviously takes a lot of time. On top of that, the manufacturer requires the interior designer to sign off on the approved sample. Doing so effectively ensures the manufacturer and, to a lesser degree, the interior designer is protected from having to eat the cost of a design error.

So, if you are as confused by the above paragraph as I was at first, my advice is to be crystal clear with clients up front – the design process and manufacturing can and often does change.

NAUGHTY WORDS

It's my opinion that there are certain words you should never use during a presentation – ever! Here is my list of naughty words:

Cheap – use inexpensive or cost effective instead

Couch – use sectional or sofa instead

Curtain – use window treatment or drapery instead

Rug – use area rug, floor covering or carpet instead

No – use yes, or it's possible instead

Is Being Vain a Thing?

Another significant consideration about presentations I feel obligated to mention is that I never took for granted (nor should anyone considering a career in interior design) that I was as much a part of a presentation as any of the high-end furnishings I was selling. An important part of my planning a presentation was always to carefully consider what to wear and how I would present myself. I believed that what I wore should be a fashion statement that reflected what I was about to present. In this case, high-end interior design. I also considered my look as another opportunity to shine – some may call this vain. It has been said that in business good shoes and good clothes open doors. I really believe this is true. Dressing well is especially important, but what's also important is expressing your own personal artistic style, creativity, and being fashionably 'up to date,' whatever that may mean to you.

Nonetheless, I knew I was being judged by clients in every aspect of our meeting including how I looked. For example, if the design I created was more on the traditional side, I dressed accordingly. And of course, don't forget the hair!

I also planned which colors I wore for a presentation, especially if I were presenting a contemporary design. Usually, patterns and colors in contemporary design are much bolder and needed to be a statement on their own. My fashion goal was to accentuate, but not distract.

SPREADING SPREADSHEET GOODNESS

From the tear sheet I would create spreadsheets; one for me, and one for the client that included product mark-ups. A mark-up is the profit margin for the showroom. The client spreadsheet had the name of the client at the top, followed by a description of the project and below that the date. Although it seems obvious, it's still worth mentioning that having the date on the spreadsheet is critical. Because if, by chance, there were any changes, meaning additions or deletions of product for example, the revised date reflected the most recent, up-to-date version of the spreadsheet. And if there was a change, it was noted on the spreadsheet by a revision number and current date. This simple notational procedure kept everyone involved in the project on the same page and helped avoid potential errors.

Separate spreadsheet columns indicate quantity, description, unit price and extended price. The unit price is per single item. The extended price is if there were multiple items. For example, if there were six chairs, I priced out the cost of one chair then totaled the six chairs together and entered it into the 'extend' column.

After all the items were entered onto the spreadsheet there was a subtotal line, sales tax line and then the total. Additionally, below the total was a line that indicated the required 50% deposit amount. Another important part of spreadsheet is a clause which clearly stated that the 50% deposit could not be canceled or refunded. On the surface, this clause might seem unreasonable. But it is important to remember that items listed on the spreadsheet were high-end, non-refundable, custom-made pieces designed specifically to a client's specifications and design plan and were in most cases essentially useless to anyone except the client.

While on the subject of spreadsheets, here are a few inside cautionary designer tips. Some might call this a bit of treachery, but I call it self-preservation. I provided clients with a copy of the spreadsheet, but intentionally omitted any overly detailed specifications. This prevented clients from doing comparison shopping and the possibility of providing leads to giving away my sources. If I believed clients were stealthily shopping around for the best deal, I would take all the product labels off and re-label items I chose to present. However, I did not object to discussing specific manufacturers because many clients, especially those with multiple homes, were familiar with and preferred high-end products.

When I first began giving presentations it took time, trial and error, and repetition to learn how to create and be successful at it. After years of presenting I was able to quickly sense whether the meeting was going well or not just a few minutes in. So will you.

HAVE INTENT, THEN PRESENT

Here's how I structured my presentations: I begin with an overview of what the client envisioned for their home. We review what each space needed, and I suggest several options and directions I might take. Then, I would describe how *I* interpreted their vision, always checking with the clients for accuracy. As their potential interior designer, I assured the clients that my goal was to create an environment to match their lifestyle. I wanted them to understand that I would create a timeless design by avoiding trends that will inevitably fade and date stamps their project. I also listened for clues during the first part of the presentation such as the mention of a piece of art they wanted me to work from, or whether their vision centered on a collaborative collection of 'sacred' items.

Next, I would explain to clients that I had chosen three different options for them to review and consider. Why three options you ask? Well, having only one option is not having an option. And although pairs are good luck, I found that two options were never enough for my clients. So, that brings us up to three, more than three and things got overwhelming and wonky. Specifically, three resplendent collections of colors and textures for my clients and I to 'play' with. Each collection had similar scale, proportion, style, and balance, but showed differences – some subtle, some dramatic.

Having three complete schemes that were different gave me another opening to illustrate my design skills and, perhaps, expand the design possibilities. I would present and explain each of the three design collections I assembled one at a time and discuss the different applications and thought processes that went into each design. The logic behind my three-option approach was to allow clients to envision how each of my schemes could possibly showcase their home. I encouraged clients to consider all three schemes, pick-and-choose, or mix-and-match from each option if they so desired.

Above all, I sought to persuade them to step outside their comfort zone and explore all the delightful directions we could possibly go. I wanted them to know there were no set rules because I did not want the clients to be intimidated by the process. Any questions they might have along the way were welcomed and addressed. After all, nothing was set in stone at this point which allowed clients to play around, edit, and take some (but not all) ownership of the presentation process. Speaking of edit, remember to always have additional options, and your trusty D.A. at the ready.

Sometimes after a big presentation I needed to review all the information several times with new clients, because there was often a lot of information to digest. The last thing you want are misunderstandings which may cause side-effects including cost over-runs, timeline setbacks, angry clients, irritability, indigestion, blurred vision, skin rash, muscle ache, stiff joints, headache, nausea, dry mouth, decreased appetite, increased sweating, nervousness, restlessness, fatigue. You get the idea.

CHAPTER 3
THE 5 Fs + L&W

I already mentioned design layers. These layers are by no means industry standard. They are simply layers I contrived using my own time-tested and seemingly shambolic logic.

1st Layer: Floor plans
2nd Layer: Flooring
3rd Layer: Furniture
4th Layer: Fabrics
5th Layer: Finishes
6th Layer: Lighting
7th Layer: Window treatments

Thus, 5 Fs + L&W

The 1st layer is the floor plan. This layer involves creating or obtaining a, hopefully, accurate floor plan drawing. Many times, clients had original floor plans of their home which was convenient and a good starting point. However, I would caution against completely trusting original floor plans because you never know if the plans you are provided included final revisions. A contractor's unnoted last-minute decision to relocate a water pipe, or electrical line could spell disaster to a plan that includes blasting through a wall to expand a room. Sometimes measurements of a room are slightly off here or there too, which can be critical to a design. Bottom line is, as the interior designer, I am ultimately responsible, so my drawings needed to be spot on!

The 2nd layer is flooring. Whether clients are keeping existing flooring, installing new flooring, or adding new area rugs, starting from the ground up is how I began my projects. Flooring is often the foundation for a plan and can be one of the most expensive items in a design or remodel budget. Just like building a house from the ground up, a solid interior design plan starts with good flooring. This is because clients are going to be seeing a lot of it, especially in large homes that may have thousands of square feet.

'THE QUESTION'

Speaking of flooring; I had a client, Grant, who needed his entire home updated and was resisting many of the options I presented. Turns out, Grant was most worried about his flooring. I knew replacing his existing flooring would be a big-ticket item, but it desperately needed to be addressed. Without any pressure from me, I asked Grant, '*The Question*'.

"Grant, can you live with it?"

I have asked many of my clients that very same question. And nine times out of ten the answer was a definite, "No. You're right. I cannot live with it."

This encouraged clients to acknowledge, out loud, to the entire world what needed to be done. *The Question* was not meant to be shaming or a judgment call, it was meant to allow the client to make the final decision without any influence or pressure from me. By the way, Grant was very happy with his new flooring.

The 3rd layer is furniture. This is when it was the showroom's time to shine. The showroom displayed several vignettes of furniture styles. Depending on the project, I utilized many of the showroom's furniture pieces as examples. In addition, I used pictures downloaded from various manufacturers the showroom represented. Using a computer tablet was a handy way to show the furniture I was suggesting.

The 4th layer is fabric. This is the part of the presentation that really captures the client's imagination and is also a favorite of mine. To me it's like opening a bottomless paint box filled with infinite color possibilities. It is also an opportunity to play with various textures and patterns. Most client's like to pick the fabrics, feel them and compare to others which I highly encouraged.

The 5th layer is finishes. Finishes can also denote style. If you think about it, every item has a finish. For example, fabrics can be shiny, antiqued, matte, or textural. Metals can be shiny, polished, hammered, antiqued, oil rubbed, matte or brushed. Many varieties of wood have different finishes; such as natural, stained, distressed (roughed and or dented), matte or polished and so on.

Another thing people overlook is that paint has a finish as well. Paint finishes can be eggshell, matte, satin, semi-gloss, or high gloss. All aspects of finishes must be considered, especially when it comes time to think about how lighting will affect a project. Many times, finishes can appear to be magnified or dulled when lighting is added to a project, which brings me to the next layer.

The 6th layer is lighting. A room lacks character without proper lighting. How can you showcase anything without sufficient lighting? It's nearly impossible. Caution though, selecting the correct color your lighting source is projecting is an important consideration. The reason being is that present day lighting sources come in an astonishing array of different colors, hues, and configurations.

For example, if you choose a light source that casts an orange, blue, or yellow shade on a green color scheme the resulting color blend will be, BARF, or permanent vision loss at the very least. Seriously though, if you run with that color scheme you have lost your vision of what your design was meant to be. Also important is the amount of natural light present in a room.

Careful attention of the manufacturing materials of lighting fixtures is another important consideration as they can also cast-off different colors and hues in a room. Also consider that the size of a fixture needs to be well scaled to the space it occupies. Nothing can be more eye-candy scrumptious than adding the perfect light fixture that defines your style, say in a foyer or dining room. Proper lighting and light fixtures can be the true shining stars in a room.

The 7th and final layer is windows – specifically window treatments. To me, window treatments were a math and engineering challenge. I never was, and still am not thrilled with doing math and I am certainly not an engineer. Nevertheless, the importance of proper window treatment is a design feature that is often overlooked or minimized. Selecting correct window treatments can help complete a room.

Let's start with drapery. Drapery options and combinations are seemingly endless; sheer, lined, patterned, pleated or plain. Drapery can have a variety of fullness depending on the thickness of your fabric. There are also options on different types of pleats.

Maybe the room needs full-on drapery treatment or just needs stationary drapery panels on either side of the window. The layout of a room's window(s) will determine whether to have the draperies center drawn, left drawn, or right drawn. Another important detail is the logical placement of the hardware that controls how to open and close both the window and window treatment.

But wait, there's more!

What about the daylight exposure to the room?

Does the drapery treatment need to be black-out?

Is there a privacy issue?

Should or can the treatments be motorized, or manually operated?

What about painted or stained wooden shutters instead of fabric?

What about vertical blinds vs. horizontal blinds?

How about a roman shade?

Does the window need a valance?

By the way, a valance is made of fabric and can be used to hide drapery hardware if desired. It can be decorative and is usually placed above the window and drapery treatment. Valances usually soften the appearance of a window treatment. They can be casual, formal, swag, layered, cascaded, or ballooned depending on the design of the room or window.

Another question is does the window need a cornice?

A cornice is similar to a valance except that it is usually made of wood. The advantage of a cornice is it can be custom designed and built into just about any shape or size imaginable. Cornices can be painted, wallpapered, or covered in fabric. A decorative trim can also be added for more embellishment.

But wait, there's even more...there's drapery hardware, such as finials that can have a variety of finishes. Finials are at the end of the drapery rod and can be made of metal, glass, wood, or acrylic. Finials are used to keep drapery fabric from slipping off the drapery rod. They can be very decorative or almost invisible. Both the drapery rod diameter and length need to be considered as well. Maybe you want the window to appear larger than it is. An easy solution is to extend the drapery hardware and drapery past the window frame to the preferred size. This little trick can enhance a room and certainly add drama. Selecting the correct style that compliments your design will pull it all together.

Consideration of the functionality and practicality is part of this whole equation of selecting beautifully designed and well-placed window treatments. With that said though, I usually did not get into too much detail about window treatments during presentations because it is very time consuming and could be a bit overwhelming for clients. Deciding on window treatments is usually done after everything else has been finalized. If a project called for drapery, it was okay to select fabrics, but that was as far as I would take it. I wanted clients to have the entire picture of what direction we were taking before moving forward with window treatments.

APOLOGIES TO LIAM NEESON

A strong word of advice – when installing any type of window treatment hire a specialist with, "… a very particular set of skills." I always hired an expert from a company that knew how to measure and install whatever application I designed and specified. I could also rely on this person for counseling or recommending solutions to the myriad of problems and challenges that can (and will) occur in a window treatment installation. For example, maybe there was not enough room to stack the draperies the way I wanted or maybe specific heavy-duty hardware was needed because of the weight and mechanics of the design. Having an expert on my team minimized these potential types of problems.

Another benefit was having the installer compile measurements and drawings. Sure, I could have done my own measuring and drawings, but having a skilled installer saved me from potential design inaccuracies. So, to avoid disaster I opted for the best insurance policy I could buy and that is, have the installer be responsible for the measurements, drawings, and installation.

Another side note – find and hire the best design workroom to create custom pieces. I had the pleasure of collaborating with LeeAnne. LeeAnne ran the best design workroom I had ever worked with. She skillfully and beautifully made all my drapery, bedding, and pillows. To say she really knew her trade was an understatement. LeeAnne was also very good at talking me down off the cliff when I was panicking because I was unsure whether I had forgotten some important detail about a project. She always gave me great advice and I trusted her completely.

To properly cover everything about window treatments would require an entire book. A handbook I do not care to write. I believe I have included enough of the main points to provide a working knowledge of the ins and outs, and ups and downs of window treatments.

CHAPTER 4
COLORS AND PATTERNS AND TEXTURES – OH MY!

Some people can memorize this or that – a poem, or a series of numbers perhaps. Curiously, I can memorize colors. I can't explain this or know of some alien oddity I might be afflicted with, but I know it's a gift, and it is a gift that keeps on giving.

Understanding color theory is a *science*. Knowing the basic color wheel and the three primary colors of red, blue, and yellow is a powerful interior design tool. Additionally, knowing how secondary colors are formed by mixing two primary colors is equally important. The traditional secondary colors are orange, purple and green.

It is commonly accepted that selecting correct colorways and various hues can influence moods and can even affect how a person feels. By the way, colorways are a range of a combination of colors. For example, a pattern can have several colorways. Maybe one colorway is in shades of blue, another might be shades of grey. In other words, the pattern remains the same, but the colorway can vary.

I often asked my clients; does a room require softer colors, like a baby's nursery? Do you want bold contrasting colors in the family room? When you have answers to these types of questions it's much easier to begin to work with colors, patterns, and textures to create interest and a cohesive design.

I understand many people don't recognize color relationships and how they can either interact or fight against each other. I found that relating color to food was an effective and simple way of defining colorways when I had a situation where a client was struggling. For example, in describing a certain shade of green I might say, "…this granny smith apple green would work well in your kitchen," or, "Have you considered a buttery yellow for the powder bath?"

Bottom line is, whether you realize it or not, everyone has a reaction to color – even in the color choices we make for our clothing and the food we buy and eat. It's an interesting and potentially important observation to notice how clients dress and the accessories they choose to wear. It can lend a clue as to what colors they are drawn to and how they wish to present themselves.

Occasionally, I used monochromatic schemes (color schemes that are a variation of one color) to add to a room depending on what I wanted to achieve. An example of a monochromatic scheme is going from pinks to reds to purples all in the same hue. This useful scheme can have soft or bright tones and various intensities of shade. Using monochromatic schemes can be a lot of fun and can also be very sophisticated if done correctly. The challenge is to not be uninteresting or predictable.

What about black? Well, I had a college teacher explain that black is the absence of color. To me it is the absence of light. I think black is powerful and presents formality and order. After all, there's a reason most formal attire is black. Of course, for some, too much black can be a bit depressing.

One of the tools I often used when playing with color was a paint deck. A paint deck is what painters use to fan through all the colors available from various paint manufacturers. If I had to work with client's existing area rug or furniture for example, I would break out my paint deck to help find a particular matching or contrasting color. Referring to the paint deck simply made it easier to pull fabrics or finishes that I needed color wise for a project.

PATTERN

Clients have asked me before, what is the rule for pattern? I tell them there is no rule. Who says you can't mix and match patterns and go a little outside your comfort zone? It's creative and interesting to have a stripe here, a geometric there, and a paisley pattern wherever. These types of combinations can delight with more visual interest. I do not want to limit clients with what can be done or force them in one certain direction.

TEXTURE

Texture adds a whole other dimension in a design. Mixing a soft velvet with a heavily woven nubby cotton creates another layer of interest. If the scheme is basically tonal and monochromatic, adding fabrics with texture creates patterns. This can be introduced in a subtle or bold way. Whenever I was selecting fabrics, I was always cognizant of how the fabric felt to the

41

touch, the application, and the fabric content – cotton versus linen for example.

If the fabric application was for a sofa, I obviously wanted a fabric that was comfortable to the touch – nothing scratchy or rough. But I also wanted the fabric to be beautiful, functional, and durable. A fabric's price-point was, at times, also a consideration depending on the client's budget.

Here is an interesting bit of trivia you can use as a 'convo' starter at your next cocktail party. The industry term for durability is 'double rubs.' Double rubs are done by a machine that goes back-and-forth over the fabric. This back-and-forth motion counts as a single double rub. The procedure tests the longevity and durability of a fabric. The number of double rubs translates into how many times people can sit on their sofa before it begins to show wear and tear. In other words, how many double rubs can you rub your can. (Yes, you read that correctly.)

Manufacturers test their fabrics and typically include notations on their labeling with appropriate applications. Overall, the fabric needs to tick all the boxes you have mentally checked, i.e., design, application, functionality, durability and sometimes availability, in order to select the perfect choice.

CHAPTER 5
WHEN IT'S ALL SAID AND ALMOST DONE

Nothing written, nothing said. No truer words have ever been said when it comes to the bottom line of an interior design budget and when money exchanges hands. After the presentation and selections finalized, the spread sheet was revised, and pricing was reviewed with the client. Because the business of interior design has a multitude of moving parts, things can potentially go awry. Revising order changes, reviewing, and finalizing the spread sheet is critical. I take that back, it's not critical, it's imperative. Also important is to verify, verify and re-verify everything. When possible, I had a colleague review my spreadsheets because once I presented it would be near impossible, not to mention awkward, to revise if an error was made.

After reviewing and editing the spreadsheet, it's important to put in writing any disclosures or important notations. When this was completed and presented to clients they were asked to sign off and submit a deposit. Getting the deposit was very exciting. Not just because of the potential money to be made, but it signaled the deal was sealed and everything I had worked so hard for was successful. Not to mention the anticipation, challenges, and excitement that came with every new project.

I always assured my clients I would take care of every detail which included, but was not limited to, handholding, hugs (for those who needed them), updates, timelines, approximate delivery dates and so on. I would let them know I consistently tracked their orders with the understanding that sometimes the universe, believe it or not, is out of my control. This is because things depended on material availability and how busy the manufacturer was when they received a sales order. Usually there was no reasons for concern, I was just practicing due diligence. I further explained that until manufactures sent back acknowledgements, I would not be able to provide firm delivery dates.

Oftentimes, there were several different manufactures working on multiple pieces for a project. So, to keep track of these types of projects, I put together what I called, not to be blasphemous, the 'project bible.' It was composed of two separate binders, one for the client and one for me. Included in the binders were spread sheets, floor plans, and pictures of all the furnishings and fixtures organized by room. My project bibles were very popular with clients. Because it was handy for them to refer to when shopping for additional items such as sheets or towels for example. I would update the project bible often so clients could be kept up-to-speed as their project progressed.

A BIBLE STORY

I had one couple who swore by the project bible – I know further unintentional blasphemy. But they used it religiously. Oops! There I go again. What follows is an adorable parable with a truly biblical ending.

Theirs was a large project with every room in the house being remodeled and refurnished. It was time we set a showroom meeting to catch up on their project-in-progress. To her misfortune, wife neglected to bring the 'bible' to the meeting. In a panic, she called her husband and pleaded with him to bring it to the showroom. Seeing an opportunity, the husband later showed up walking in with an actual copy of *the* Holy Bible in hand. This caught the attention and was well received as quite a clever joke by the showroom staff. Wife, on the other hand, was not amused and roundly scolded him for being a wise guy. Luckily, he brought both with him. Praise be to hubby!

CHAPTER 6
CONTRACTORS & REPS

Engaging excellent contractors! Geez Louise, I cannot say enough, but I will try. When pricing out a remodel or new build, obtaining two or three bids is of vital importance. When I had a project that required a contractor, I would invite several contractors on-site to bid – at the same time. This may sound counter-intuitive, brash, and a bit treacherous, but having multiple contractors onsite kept them honest. Another benefit – contractors see their competition. Plus, I only had to explain a project and answer questions once. And, in a perfect world, everyone would be on the same page. Personally, I felt it was the fairest and most efficient way to get my bids. Also, if contractors had follow-up questions after our initial on-site meeting, I would level the process by emailing back each contractor my response so I could compare bids that would address the question – comparing apples to apples so to speak.

Never hesitate to ask contractors the following when comparing bids;

Why is one bid or section less costly than another?

Why is one higher than the other?

I would also ask myself;

Could it be the contractor's bid, or did I overlook something in the plans?

Can this contractor work to my timeline and get it done according to the plans and all the specifications?

Can this contractor provide professional references, samples of work, and customer testimonials?

It was my responsibility to ensure contractors were able to complete their mission without my constant supervision. That doesn't mean I am not inspecting their work, but at the same time there could be several projects that required my attention, so it was important to hire a contractor that was dependable.

It is important to remember that contractors are not mind readers. You can walk and talk the project with them, but in the end, contractors need documentation, schedules, and direction. Naturally, communication is crucial, and part of my job is to provide that. One of my mantras when working with contractors was, 'Nothing written, nothing said.' I always stored documentation including change orders, revisions, emails, and meeting notes on hand with copies I could distribute, if needed, that made sure everyone was on the same page. This saved me and my clients a lot of time and reduced the chances of painful revisions. I was diligent about keeping records of everything, especially in the event there was a misunderstanding, mistake, or delay. On a side note, if a piece of custom furniture was delivered and was fabricated incorrectly, my records became verification whether it was my fault or the manufacturers'.

Texting was a quick and easy tool I frequently utilized. Proceed with caution though as the tone of text messages, and emails for that matter, can be easily misinterpreted. As the interior designer, I knew the buck stopped with me. I was responsible for compiling pricing, scheduling, floor plans, defining demolition, and sometimes keeping track of materials needed for a project. Being able to relay various communications between all parties, all while being organized, consistent, and time-sensitive, was another hat I wore.

Practicing interior design had more details and moving parts than I could possibly imagine, particularly when I first stepped foot in this business. Forgetting to specify, or omitting a single item a contractor needed from my spread sheet or floor plan could foul up everything. By the time it took to find, order, and receive replacement materials, or substitute items, it would set off a chain reaction that often-had dire consequences. Not to mention the strong possibility that an item had an extended lead time, been discontinued or was unavailable within the project's time frame and budget. The last thing I wanted was animosity with my contractor or clients. My priority was preventing my professionalism or my authority to come into question. After all, who likes admitting to an oversight? I avoided said slipups at all costs, and there is no doubt in my mind that precise, accurate, current, and double-checked documentation was invaluable.

JAN THE MAN

I was fortunate enough to work with Jan, an extraordinary general contractor. Jan was a seasoned vet and had recruited a team of excellent trades people that were on her payroll. She was organized, communicative, and very knowledgeable of products and the construction industry as a whole. She also had considerable experience working with interior designers, a notable bonus as this was not always the case. More often than not, general contractors subcontract their work to a tradesperson they often don't even know. Jan's core team of trades people on the other hand, instilled her accountability for their work. The quality of work done by her trades people was a direct reflection of her and because of this she was reliable, accessible, and very particular. My experience with Jan and her team ensured me that projects progressed efficiently and that team members were informed and well-versed. They communicated well with each other when a project was ready for the next phase, thus saving time and cost over-runs.

FOR THE LOVE OF REPS

Manufacturer sales representatives or reps can be either friend or foe. I aimed to create strong relationship with reps when it came to products I truly loved and chose for my projects.

As far as the foes were concerned, well, who wants enemies at work? Occasionally there were sales reps who did not respond in a timely manner or not respond at all for that matter. Sometimes they provided me inaccurate delivery dates, gave me incomplete or misrepresented information about a product, or were just plain lazy – quite annoying and inexcusable if you ask me.

On the other hand, sales reps that spend time in the showroom educating interior designers are, in my opinion, elite. Most of the professional reps I worked with were very knowledgeable of the product lines they represented. They know the interior design world is tight knit with infinite competition. Meaning, if the product was everything it promised to be, it would ignite and rise to the top as a coveted item. On the other hand, if a product was a stinker, news of its stench spread like wildfire and no one in their right mind would touch it. Obviously, sales reps and interior designers did not want that to happen because reputations are so highly coveted.

Fortunately for me, most of the products I sought after for specific projects were high-end lines. Quality was priority for me and my clients, and I knew the sales reps and manufacturers I specified would stand behind their products.

Part of a sales rep's job was to introduce new products, and ensure samples and catalogs were current, and educate interior designers on all components of the product. However, if I had a question on production, meaning which stage an item was in the manufacturing process, with their blessing I often bypassed the rep and spoke directly with the manufacturer.

Knowledge is power, and the more I understood the workings and qualities of a product, the better I was equipped to recommend and sell it. My bestie sales reps explained to me the details about material, design, and quality of the piece which gave me the confidence to present their products to a client. Many manufacturers will also invite interior designers to visit their factory and showrooms. It's a valuable tool to know and see how a product is crafted from the ground up. It further instilled confidence in me to recommend a manufacturer when I understood how their product line was built.

CHAPTER 7
INSTALLATION

Installation – the end of the project trail. It involves pulling together and orchestrating all the moving parts of a project. Installations meant anticipation and sometimes fear.

Before I launch into the installation process though, I am compelled to say that I was very fortunate to have several projects in progress at the same time. This fortune was a double-edged sword however, because at times it resulted in organized chaos. It goes without saying that it is not always easy to organize chaos. When it came time to arranging an installation, I invaded every inch of flat surface in the showroom I could, including the floor. Yes, the floor works surprisingly well when spreading out project details for review before setting out to begin an installation. My organized chaos method does not work for everyone and sometimes drove my coworkers bonkers, but it worked for me.

I learned that the key to organizing chaos is keep things simple. With that, I kept all my files and client specific information in their own personalized bins. Inside their cozy bin lived a file folder with the name of each room, its floor plan, pictures of the furniture, finishes, and fabric samples and so on. I always kept my bins close by and consistently up to date so that when a project was to be installed, I was fully prepared.

As product trickled in for a project's installation, I preferred to inspect the delivery if possible. Our design firm contracted an offsite shipping and receiving warehouse company not far from our showroom. It was the responsibility of the warehouse associates to inspect the larger pieces the showroom could not always receive directly, for example large upholstered pieces, case goods and hefty light fixtures.

Items can often shift in containers during shipment which may cause damage. If the product arrived damaged, the warehouse manager would email me pictures of all signs of the damage, and I would go to the warehouse and inspect. Sometimes it was an easy fix or repair – and sometimes not. Retaining a skilled and dependable repair person is highly desirable and quite important.

Prepping for an installation demanded time, scheduling, organization and thought to align all the moving parts that needed to be in place. When we were ready to install, I would take the trusty project bin and set up an area in the home where I was able to pull folders and direct my installers where to place each item. I found this method of organization decreased a significant amount of stress during the installation and moved things along efficiently. Occasionally, some of the team would wander over and look at the piles of project related paperwork scattered here and there and shake their heads. I know they were tempted to look, but I made it very clear, "Don't even think about touching my chaos!"

They got the message.

This installation comes to mind when I think about organization. The project was to accessorize a large and beautiful contemporary home. The home's owner, Sheila, had most of her furniture and explained to me that she was eager to put the finishing touches on her home before they left for the summer. She and her husband Lance split their time between two large homes.

Of course, I had visited their home previously and knew the layout, the colors, and the style Sheila was after. I spent hours in the showroom selecting and preparing all the items I knew would work in their home with the usual extra accessories as back up. There was no time to go through catalogs, do additional shopping or hunt through exclusive websites for items because of their impending departure. I was confident I had everything I wanted from the showroom to complete the project.

I had two installers and a design assistant to help me. This house was humungous, so I needed all the help I could get, plus I had to move quickly as they were on a time crunch to embark on their summer travel.

One quick side note, I was never afraid to ask for help. Whether it be an installation, a presentation, my mental health, or how to manage eccentric clients. I discovered that in the long run it benefitted me, my clients, and the company as well to ask for help.

Back to Sheila's install. We arrived in a large van and an SUV loaded to the gills with accessories. When Sheila greeted me at the door I walked in and

introduced my team. And then I invoked *the* rule –
'You must now leave your home,' delivered with a wry
smile of course. Sheila got the biggest grin and asked,
"Okay, what kind of music would you like while we
are gone?"

Sheila and Lance were good sports and happily left
us to do what we do while Baroque music played softly
throughout the house. I let her know I would text her
when we were finished.

Once they left, I gave my team a quick tour then
began unloading boxed and blanket wrapped items. We
had thick drop cloths spread out in the foyer where we
staged everything. I got to work placing various
accessories, artwork, a few pieces of furniture, plants
and light fixtures of all sizes and shapes throughout the
home. I went through the house several times adding
items, moving things around, and sometimes removing
existing items. *'Noodling'* as I call it, until it all felt
right to me. Fortunately, not many of their existing
items were sacred, so I had the freedom to do what I
thought looked best.

After a few hours I notified Sheila that we were
ready for the big reveal. She quickly responded and I
told them to enter through the foyer to begin their tour.
I led the way explaining briefly what I had added to
each room and explained my inspiration and thought
process. Lance and Sheila were nerve-racking silent
the entire time while they listened, nodded their heads,
and observed everything intently as we walked through
their home.

When my tour was complete, I politely stepped
aside so Sheila and Lance could chat about what they
had seen. After what seemed like an eternity, Sheila

walked over to me, straight-faced, and said, "We absolutely love it, we will take it all!"

HALLELUIAH! It was always an incomparable thrill and, I'll say it, an elated ego-boost for me when I saw excitement and appreciation in the work I had done for my clients. These types of experiences were almost euphoric and, frankly, what kept me going for the rest of the day and beyond.

CODE RED – TIME FOR SOME MORE DIRT

The trouble began the instant *they* walked into the showroom. I greeted *them* and introduced myself. *They* awkwardly proceeded to do the same, "I'm Beth and this is my husband, Daniel."

No hellos or, nice to meet you from this pair! Instead, Beth quite brusquely announced, "We know exactly what bedroom furniture we want. Let's get right to it. We'd prefer you didn't waste our time."

My jaw dropped, but she wasn't done, "Do you price match?" she asked.

Immediately an alarm bell went off in my head – CODE RED! Danger ahead! Proceed with caution. I did my best to recover from her frosty onslaught, but all I could do was respond, "Ahh, um, yes, we can price match."

I took a moment to regain my composure and invited them to have a seat at a table just outside my office. Beth then proceeded to show me pictures and price tags of items she liked from another store. Oh-oh! Code red number two! I hastened to make a mental note-to-self at that point – she was price comparing and this may not be a good thing. A little voice inside my

56

head was warning me to be on guard. I struggled to quiet the warnings, and the distracting little voice inside my head. To add to my distraction I was conflicted.

My conscience was telling me, "Julie, do not be judgmental. You need to remain professional. Plus, you need this sale."

But I still couldn't stop the little voice from quietly repeating, "You'll be sorrr-eeeey!" in the back of my head.

Although these two undoubtedly needed an etiquette lesson, they certainly knew their furnishings. I instantly recognized the manufacturer from the pictures Beth had with her. The pieces were clearly the Ferrari of furniture. I now realized that gaining Beth and Daniel's business would be a large order resulting in a sizeable profit, in other words, a big payday for me. So, with that nagging little voice still in the back of my mind, and against my better judgment, I wrote down the items they wanted. The list included a king-size headboard, two nightstands, a nine-drawer dresser, accent side table and a bedroom chaise.

I had very little to do with the selection of actual furniture pieces they had previously shopped for and found. Instinctively, I knew I should play it close-to-the-vest with these two, so I decided to pull large boards loaded with the manufacturer's wood finishes and racks of fabric to be absolutely sure we had the correct colors for the pieces they had previously chosen. What made me even more anxious though is that it's not always possible to distinguish exact finishes and colors from a photo, even if photographed professionally. More importantly, I certainly did not want to be guessing about items in my dealings with this 'dangerous duo' – not even an educated guess.

After spending several rather dicey, touch-and-go hours with Beth and Daniel they appeared to be pleased and finalized their selections. I then found all their items in our catalogues and priced them accordingly to match our competitor. In a CYA (look it up if you must) moment I thought, 'I need to protect myself.' So, I recanted everything that took place between Beth and Daniel to the showroom's owner, got his assurance and buy-in. Only then did I proceed to gather and complete the necessary paperwork for their order.

The last detail to wrap this deal up was for me to write everything up on a sales order, review it with Beth and Daniel and get their 50% deposit. But wait a minute! Now it was husband Daniel's turn to stun me by requesting that he wanted a discount for paying for everything with cash.

"Okay, we can do that," I said.

But wait, he also wanted an additional discount in the event they did not receive their furniture when they wanted. After some painfully awkward discussion we finally came to terms and I had them sign off on the sales order and warily collected their 50% deposit.

The product finally arrived – and on time thank goodness! I asked our chosen freight line to collect the crated furniture that had arrived from overseas. I also arranged a delivery date and time with Beth and Daniel.

When I arrived at Beth and Daniel's home the delivery driver and his helper had begun to uncrate the furniture. Each piece of furniture was unwrapped and staged on furniture blankets in the client's driveway so I could carefully inspect each item. Turns out, while in transit the furniture bypassed the manufacturer's receiving warehouse and, as a result, had never been inspected prior to arriving at Beth and Daniel's. 'This could be trouble,' I thought, because one of the inspections that usually occurred, did not. And it *was* trouble. Beth and Daniel's furniture had tiny scratches and imperfections. Luckily though, the delivery driver had a furniture touch up kit, so I was able to take care of detailing the pieces that needed a little TLC.

Warning – touch up repairs can be complicated. What I'm getting at is the dilemma of whether I should point out every little flaw to a client when a delivery arrives? Well, usually I didn't, unless there was serious damage. Why, because if anyone has the determination, even if they were inspecting the Hope diamond, they will undoubtedly find little scratches and tiny imperfections. Also if you begin to fret over minor flaws with clients, they will begin to question everything, get upset, and may proceed to scrutinize, crawl all over, and inspect every little detail. If this happens, you are no longer in the driver's seat. Your delivery and installation have gone sideways. I'm not saying you should be deceitful, but no product is perfect. Human beings are building, manufacturing, assembling, packing, and unpacking products and are bound to be unwittingly careless at times – sometimes things just happen. With that said, before placing imperfect furniture I would take precautionary pictures and notify my office. I would explain the repairs I had made and that I was satisfied that everything was looking good, or not.

Back to Beth and Daniel's install – when we finished placing everything and I was satisfied with how all the pieces looked, Beth and Daniel came into their bedroom and were delighted. I collected the balance and told them if I could be of further assistance, they could call me.

Surprisingly – and I do mean the good kind of surprise – that evening I was bombarded with texts from Beth thanking me for taking such good care of them and how happy they were. I was happy too, until the following day when Beth and Daniel made a complete 180-degree turnaround from the couple that, the night before, gushed over how happy they were. Beth called me and it was like listening to a completely different person. She was verbally assaulting, spewing expletives, and accusing me of selling and delivering defective furniture.

Man was she furious. She did not mention anything about the touch up I had made – she just continued her rampage. Besides, the touch ups I made were miniscule, and only visible under a magnifying glass. She made it sound as though there were huge gouges in the furniture and that the repairs were made using mud from their front lawn. When I finally was able to settle her down, I told her I would contact the sales rep and get things resolved to her satisfaction.

To make a long story even longer, the sales rep came out and inspected the furniture and told Beth and Daniel all the pieces looked good. They vehemently disagreed. To my disbelief, they insisted on yet another discount. For the love of all creatures great and small! Cash discount, delivery discount, now an alleged damage discount! Enough already! Was I upset?

Wouldn't you be? First and foremost, I wanted my clients to be happy and obviously in this situation they were not. Besides, discounts cut into profit, which cut into commission which, in turn, took money out of my pocket.

Nonetheless, I knew these clients were not going to go away. I also knew that if we denied them a discount the showroom and manufacturer would suffer. So, we gave them the discount. In fact, there were more discounts in this deal than I had ever experienced. I also believe that once the clients suspected minor repairs or touch ups had been made, they ran with it with the intention of getting something for next to nothing – disgraceful, IMHO.

RUTHIE'S AREA RUG RAGE – WE'RE TALKING TURKEY HERE

One final behind the scenes story; my new client Ruth was looking for an area rug for her den. In all the time I spent with her, I don't think I ever saw Ruth smile even once or show me any happiness for that matter. The only explanation I could think of for Ruth's demeanor is that she may have been prescribed daily doses of vinegar. One thing Ruth did have was a den festooned with a very interesting collection of tribal art, sculptures, and wooden carvings she and her husband had collected in their travels. She wanted to complete her tribal den by adding an area rug.

I had some area rugs in mind and showed her various handmade samples from Turkey. My thought was the natural, organic quality of a handmade area rug would meld perfectly with her eclectic collection.

However, I also cautioned her that exact color matching of handmade, hand-knotted area rugs made overseas can be a challenge. In hindsight, my cautionary advisement might have been a mistake.

Nevertheless, Ruth settled on a very simple geometric design in black and cream. I placed an order for an 8 x 10-foot area rug and received it within a few days. Ruth was eager for me to deliver and install it, so three of us from the showroom went up to Ruth's to move her furniture and place the area rug. Immediately Ruth began to complain that the new area rug was not the same as the sample I had previously shown her. I explained the 2 x 3-foot sample was just that – a sample. I again reminded Ruth that the area rug was hand-knotted in Turkey, and dye lots, although very close to the samples, are not always spot on. In my opinion, this is the beauty of a handmade rug; no two are exactly the same.

But Ruth continued to remain un-satisfied. She wanted her area rug to be exactly like the sample. So, I contacted our sales rep and begged her to, please, initiate a country-wide APB to try and find a match. Next thing you know we had area rugs shipped in from New York, Dallas, Los Angeles, the Congo, Mars – you name it.

All the area rugs were spectacular, but sadly none were exactly like the 2 x 3-foot sample. Every time we received a new shipment, I invited Ruth and her husband to come to the showroom with the hope that the area rug would meet their approval. To no avail, as nothing we had shipped in pleased her. As a last resort, I had the sales rep speak to Ruth in hopes to, once again, educate her on the unscientific process of

Turkish dying and knotting area rug making – talking Turkey in other words. She didn't exactly like her lesson. Oh, what to do, what to do?

While Ruth, her husband, our sales rep, and I were in the showroom we spied a black and cream area rug in Ruth's pattern that had just been delivered. When I saw this area rug, I knew it was a good match, but at 9 x 12-feet, it was larger than Ruth had wanted. Nevertheless, Ruth grabbed the sample and said that she thought it was a good match and asked if we would take it up to her home.

When we placed the 9 x 12-foot area rug, Ruth was pleased, and with a few furniture adjustments the size worked as well. I was so relieved and hoped the whole episode was over and done. Was this to be the end of Ruth's Rug Rage?

Of course not, we're just getting started here. I informed Ruth that the larger 9 x 12-foot area rug was more expensive than the 8 x 10-foot area rug she ordered. Ruth wasn't done bringing the pain though as she demanded she would keep the larger area rug and announced,

"I WILL NOT, UNDER ANY CIRCUMSTANCE, PAY THE DIFFERENCE IN PRICE!"
Everyone present, including her husband, was astonished. I was worried she had suddenly become possessed and her head was going to spin 360-degrees demon-like.

Yes. I can admit it. Ruth was mildly inconvenienced during the time it took to find a replacement area rug, but her outrageous behavior and terms just did not seem well-placed in my view. 'Why would she pull the area rug out from under me?' I thought. (Yes, admittedly shameful jeu de mots…). If Ruth only knew to what extent my team, our sales rep, and other showrooms had all gone through. That they all spent an enormous amount of time and effort searching for just the *right* area rug, maybe then she would agree to pay the difference. But deep down I knew Ruth would claim, 'It's not my problem, nor do I care.'

Well, I called the showroom owner, and being one to take the path of least resistance and not wanting to lose the sale, he told me, "Let her keep the area rug, don't charge her the difference."

Wow… just like that, the saga of Ruthie's Rug Rage was over.

But the whole episode didn't quite sit with me; in fact it gnawed, and apparently continues to gnaw at me. Sometimes, I just don't know how people live with themselves when they practice this brand of duplicity. I guess in her mind she believed she was entitled in some way. But when I try to reconcile her behavior and the fact that she should claim possession of the larger area rug costing thousands of dollars more than she paid, it just didn't seem right to me.

Ah, but I got over it. Happy to turn the page on that day and take a valuable lesson home that even though it may seem ultra-mind-numbing, it's vitally important to explain in agonizing detail dye lots and the imperfections, uniqueness, and beauty of handmade, hand-knotted area rugs to clients. It's kind of a tedious and seemingly trivial matter, but one that over time became near and dear to my heart.

To sum up and get back on a positive trajectory let me finish by saying that I had very few experiences like Ruthie's Rug Rage. For that I am grateful and count myself lucky, lucky, lucky.

CHAPTER 8
INSTALLING ACCESSORIES – ARTFUL MOVES

Installing accessories was one of my favorite parts of a project. It was the project's jewelry, and I love, love, love jewelry. It was when everything came together. It was my time to explore and present possibilities, even in the tiniest detail. It was the time to make artful moves.

Preparing for an accessory installation involved visiting the client's home in advance and perhaps doing a little measuring, particularly if there was shelving, art, or an area rug. Sometimes the products I wanted to place were already in the showroom – Score! Other times, I had to research to find the perfect piece. When it came to accessorizing, clients always seemed to want everything instantaneously.

Occasionally I had projects that all that was needed was a few accessories to make a home sizzle. It did not matter if the project was large or small. Sometimes all it took to put the finishing touches on a room was to simply move existing pieces around in the space. Reset the room if you will. Maybe remove pieces (making sure items were not 'sacred') to open up the space, re-hang a piece of art in a different location, and then we refresh with new accessories. Many times, I had to weave in client's personal items with new items I brought to the party. This was usually not a problem though.

BALANCING THE SCALES OF INTERIOR DESIGN JUSTICE

Understanding scale and balance in working with all sizes and shapes of accessories is essential. Scale is finding the correct proportion and relation to the size of the room and its existing features. Balance is having a good sense of how the objects are working together in design placement. Gaining that sense takes time and experience but, there are short cuts (more about short cuts to come). Basically, my goal and design philosophy was to make everything shine, make it interesting, and make it unpredictable. Yes, you read that correctly, unpredictable, because that too involves design skill and an eye for intrigue.

MAKE CLIENTS DISAPPEAR

One of my best kept secrets, until now, is that when I went to my client's home for an accessory installation, I made them leave the room. Surprisingly, every client I worked with went along with this request. Not once did I experience resistance or push back. In fact, clients loved the anticipation and mystery behind my request. Why not make it fun? My reasoning for this strange request was simply that I worked better without a client hovering and watching over me. Besides, I had little tricks and secrets I had developed over the years that I did not want to share. I wanted complete freedom to move things around, study the layout and objects I was working with. It was far better for me when there were no distractions from the magic I needed to conjure to make the room come alive.

Not until I was finished and convinced my magic spell had taken hold, when I knew the pieces I worked with settled into their new home did I invite clients back in. My favorite part was the look on their faces as they scanned the room. The delighted expressions looked like they had just walked in on a surprise party on their behalf. Others claimed it was as though they had magically stepped into the home they had always dreamed about. Clients really enjoyed seeing their new look for the first time. It was worth everything to me as an interior designer to see, feel, and share their excitement. Rarely was there a word spoken. Their endorsement was expressed through pure delight. I did not consider my project a success until I felt their satisfaction.

Odd Man In! - And Other Super-Secrets

Another design approach I found that worked well was numerology, specifically using odd numbers as a technique when placing accessories. Arranging objects in odd numbers often lead to asymmetrical groupings. Asymmetry, if done correctly, brings interest and something unexpected. Symmetry can, of course, be used as well. It just depended on the look I was trying to achieve for the client.

Part of gaining artful moves is being able to relate new accessories to existing colors that you may have to accept and work with in the home. This can be especially challenging when selecting and placing accessories. The challenge is making sure that what you have selected works with what is already present. Not always an easy task.

Here's another tip. If the room's existing color is yellow for example, using the opposite of yellow on the color wheel can be fun and will make accessories pop. The complementary color of yellow is violet, which is a secondary color on the color wheel. Utilizing complementary colors that contrast each other makes a powerful statement.

One of the advantages of working in a showroom was I had an almost endless resource of accessories including art, sculptures, plants, small pieces of furniture, lamps, or an étagère – a what? Okay, I'm showing off its just posh shelving. Sometimes even area rugs can be an accessory used to anchor a room and make a statement. Perhaps the foyer needed a large colorful vase, or decorative mirror to announce a little drama when entering the home.

This may seem obvious, but I would like to point out that items will appear differently in the client's home than in the showroom. Colors cast a completely different hue due to the synthetic quality and harshness of showroom finishes and textures under commercial lighting. So, keep that in mind.

Bottom line is, depending on the design and desired finished look, with the correct accessories you can shout or whisper the room's design. Making artful moves when installing accessories has the effect of pulling together loose ends.

CHAPTER 9
TOOLS OF THE TRADE – IT'S IN THE BAG

My go-to designer's tool bag was a well-used, thick plain black canvas bag that contained things constantly in use and what I now consider to be sentimental. The tool bag was always standing at attention in the corner of my office patiently waiting to be called to duty. My tool bag was strictly off limits to everyone, and I mean everyone. That was because before my embargo, the things inside the bag were often 'borrowed' by my colleagues and had a way of disappearing never to return. It was my tool belt, and I used these tools of the trade constantly – particularly when I went to a home for the first time, or on an installation.

Being prepared was forever essential when out in the field. Here is a list of the tools I always had with me:

- Painter's tape
- Pad of graph paper, pens & pencils
- Floor plans (when available)
- Two measuring tapes
- Project bins (all samples)
- Architectural scale
- Batteries
- Extension cords
- Touch up kit – markers or liquid finish
- Small Toolbox

Not just any small toolbox, mind you. I searched for a very specific toolbox. It was a shamelessly 'girly' brightly colored teal toolbox whose colorful purpose was to scare off macho contractor dudes from helping themselves to tools they needed but forgot to bring to the jobsite. It's outward appearance effectively camouflaged its very useful contents including one-sided razor blades, a box cutter, scissors, various sizes of nails, brads and other hardware, a small hammer, screwdrivers with various head sizes, pliers, a level, carpenter's glue, stick-on moleskin furniture pads of all sizes, and a small ruler.

Oh, and don't forget to bring along a camera or a cell phone which can be used to take photos of finished installations for a portfolio or to upload to social media. A camera or cell phone is also useful for photographically documenting any damage that may have occurred to furniture prior to installation.

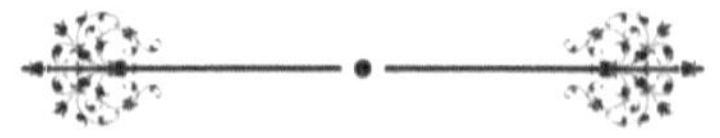

CHAPTER 10
SALES SCHMALES

The definition of a salesperson is: A person whose job is to sell a product or service in a given territory, in a store, or by telephone.

Sales? Yuck! When I went to school we never talked about sales! We were artists after all and sales…no thank you. My apologies for the stereotype, but the first thing that comes to mind when I think salesperson, is a pushy, shady man trying to sell me a car for much more than it's worth. The point is, I did not sign up for salesmanship. Naively, I thought, I'm a rock-star designer, they're all going to flock to me and love, love, love my work because I'm charming and great at what I do. Sales schmales!

Well, I am here to tell you in the interior design business it's much more complicated and goes considerably beyond artistic talent alone. As I explained earlier on, it is both business and personal. Salesmanship in the interior design world is a skill that takes considerable practice and experience. You are selling yourself as a well-educated and savvy expert professional first. You also need to have a thorough knowledge of design products, a clear sense of your customer base, and the vision and understanding of the design firm, or your own individual vision if you own your own design firm.

Most of all you must love what you do. The interior design business is very competitive and multi-layered, important reasons why I loved the work. There was also the endless combination of clients' personalities, homes, projects, and products that was always fascinating and a challenge.

As I said, learning to become a good salesperson and experimenting with what works in a variety of situations takes experience and a great deal of patience. A gentle, sophisticated sales technique that worked for me was to offer the option of bringing various items to a client's home. This option was especially effective when clients were having a difficult time visualizing what items will look like in their home. I would deliver and supervise the placement of several items so clients could physically see how they transformed a room. Providing this option had the added benefit of eliminating the inconvenience of clients having to load and unload showroom pieces back and forth.

For example, when I selected and brought area rugs or accessories and placed them in a client's home, they felt comfortable with the process. Why? Well, to begin, there was no financial commitment on their part. I did not charge for trying it on for size. I found this to be an excellent passive approach to salesmanship. Besides, it was easier to sell product when it's physically in a client's home. After all, it is hard to say "no" to a piece that is perfection when items simply spoke for themselves.

What can I say except, 'when its right it's right!' And when I knew I had the perfect piece for a particular room, there was rarely any further discussion. Once a client saw the benefit and ease of working with a professional interior designer, it typically got them excited and motivated them to push on with a project. Often, clients simply needed objective professional advice to place the finishing touches on their home.

REFERRAL MADNESS

The following anecdote is about the importance of referrals. I was fortunate to have many referrals, but I like this one in particular. Linda and Steve were very dear clients of mine. One day Linda called me and said she had recommended me to her best friends, Kelly and Tom. They were visiting and admired the work I had done in Linda and Steve's second home. Kelly and Tom had just purchased a second home not too far from Linda and Steve and needed interior design services.

Linda and I had a wonderful relationship and she was kind enough to give me a little insight into their friend's likes and dislikes. Linda's inside info helped me learn a little history about their relationship as they were newly married and combining their treasures.

I believe receiving a referral is one of the biggest compliments an interior designer can receive, and in this case, it was as though my work had sold itself even before I had met them. Sure, I still had to work at getting to know this couple and their dreams, but I had a leg up and an invite into their home. With Linda's keen insight I was able to move forward quickly in pulling Kelly and Tom's project together.

UP, UP-SELL, AND AWAY

Here's a story about a subtle way to up-sell. I think of it as up-selling with purpose. It had been a while since

Diane had come into the showroom. Ironically, that morning I picked up her file folder and skimmed over my notes wondering when she would, again, grace me with her presence. I had completed several projects for her in the past, and she had a new project she had been telling me about for months.

Out of the blue, Diane turned up at the showroom and told me she was now ready to proceed. We chatted briefly about what she wanted while we strolled around the showroom. I visualized her home and remembered a huge wall in the living room with a very large TV situated dead center. From the get-go I had a feeling Diane was not happy that the TV was the star of the beautiful room we had completed just months earlier. In fact, she was quite upset telling me, "Every time I walk by this room all I see is a giant, blank, black screen." She added that she felt the room needed some additional artwork and a few accessories.

I thought about her problem for a few minutes while we continued to stroll around the showroom. Then it came to me. I suggested we design and build a stunning custom-made picture frame for the TV. She was hesitant at first thinking that adding a custom frame would only bring more attention to the already giant black hole of a TV screen. On top of that, after looking through catalogs she didn't like any of the frame examples the showroom offered. She asked if she could have more choices.

"Yes, of course," I answered. I didn't know where I was going to find them, but that was my problem and "Yes" should always be the response.

"Here's what I'm also thinking," I told Diane. "You can insert a flash drive into the TV with a variety of images that interest you."

In other words, her normally dormant TV screen would display an ever-changing array of anything she liked. She could even customize the flash drive to display artwork, family pictures, or photos of trips she and her husband had taken. The possibilities were endless.

This got Diane very excited, and she now saw a solution to her TV screen displeasure. Providing these types of options is a simple, yet effective example of creative up-selling. I did eventually locate a suitable frame for Diane, and I let her know she could take it a step further by layering the frame and adding colorful mats and liners. This is another fine example of up-selling and giving the client more than they were expecting or hoping for. I also helped Diane choose several pieces of art and a few accessories that I thought would be perfect.

Her reaction, "They're mine!"

Diane's next question was, could I customize the framing because she wanted something more ornate for the art pieces. My response was, "Absolutely."

My point is, I always say yes first. Yes, I can make it happen. Yes, there is a price for this. Yes, this may take time. However, when the client is getting what they want, costs and delays are generally not an issue. Yes, is a powerful, positive word and if my clients or I can imagine it, then, yes, I can create it. There you have it, up-selling with a purpose.

Cathy called from the Midwest and told me her realtor recommended me. She and her husband David had just purchased a second home and needed help. We had an immediate connection as I listened to her animated and excited voice. She wanted to get started on her new home right away. This was a case of, I want it, and I want it now; will you please help? So as not to delay the project I told Cathy we could communicate by video conferencing, email, text, and phone. She assured me she would be open and accessible to my plan.

Cathy and her husband were not coming out for several weeks and wanted to get a head start on furnishings. So, Cathy told me her property manager would give me access so that I could see her home. She further explained what she envisioned for the home, which was brand new construction and very contemporary. Obviously, her furnishings were to be contemporary, and she wanted the colors to be neutrals in layers of grey.

Although I felt rushed and already under pressure I immediately contacted the property manager and requested an appointment. I knew after reviewing the real estate website of this newly built home that it had spectacular views, amazing architecture, and finishes, and that it would be a fantastic project.

Of course, I jumped on board immediately. I knew this project would require two assistants as it was a very large home. Time was of the essence as my new clients were on a fast track to get things shipshape. The good thing was the home was completely empty, so I had a blank canvas to work with. Plus, I had beautiful, tonal neutral finishes to work with. Luckily, furniture right off the showroom floor would be perfect, and it was exactly what I had in mind.

My design assistants and I spent several hours touring the home, taking pictures, and measuring the interior, and the enormous outside deck. I was certain the home's spectacular outdoor living space would require exceptional contemporary furnishings as well, which presented a possible up-sell opportunity.

The three of us gathered what we needed and adjourned to the showroom. I began to study the photos of their home, plus all the notes I had taken and immediately started designing in my head. Meanwhile, my team drew up CAD floor plans. I soon had a direction, or I should say several directions for this project. One of the design assistants and I began pulling pictures of furnishings and fabrics and layered them accordingly along with floor plans.

After a couple days of planning, I called Cathy from the showroom and told her I was ready to give a presentation via video conferencing. I meticulously went through each room explaining the floor plan options with all the materials I had pulled. During the presentation I took a moment to walk around the showroom and point out many furnishings that would work perfectly. The beauty in doing this was, with her long-distance approval I could immediately begin installing the beautiful new furnishings she chose. Cathy and I went back and forth on a few items, but overall, the presentation went well, and she was excited for me to move forward.

What I wish to point out about this project is the importance phone manners and tone of voice can make a genuine difference and impression when dealing with very long-distance clients.

Another important note about this project is that the use of technology is a viable and efficient way to collaborate with out of state clients. Working with Cathy and David via email, phone, and video conferencing for most of the project was a great experience. In fact, Cathy, and her husband's entire project was pretty much done sight-unseen using technology only. Overall, the project was relatively stress free, things moved quickly, and I was able to come and go into their home and do my work as needed which was an added bonus. I also installed most of the fabulous artwork throughout their home via our video chats. We did eventually meet face-to-face when the project was nearly complete. They were both truly a delight and incredibly pleased with the result.

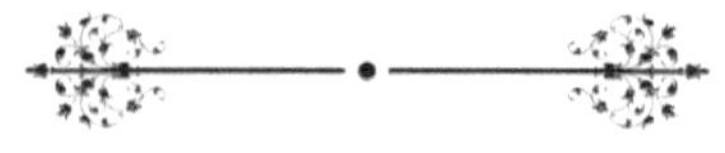

CHAPTER 11
VAMPIRES AND OTHER SHENANIGANS

IT'S HARD TO B-POSITIVE AROUND VAMPIRES

Before we forge ahead, I want to warn you about a couple of classifications in the industry for various types of clients interior designers encounter, one type being vampires. Watch out for vampires! And be warned, none of the traditional methods used to repel vampires – garlic, silver bullets, mirrors, wooden stakes, incantations – do not work against vampire clients.

Being a seasoned interior designer, I was usually able to read people and identify vampires, or 'tire-kickers' as they are also called, when I saw them. I initially gave those who visited the showroom the benefit of the doubt, but as things developed, I would steer clients toward the understanding that our relationship must be built on trust.

This is another reason I believe spending time and getting to know clients is really important. I felt that they needed to trust me before I could give them my best and guide them through the process of the design and, ultimately, a completed project.

There are several species of client vampires, the first being those who pose as clients but are only there to steal your ideas and use them as their own. Be warned that giving too much information before establishing the extent of a project and before being hired is not a good thing. It is a red flag when clients start asking countless questions about the finite details of a product or any sources before any contract is signed. I can cite instances when customers would visit the showroom, feign interest, gather the information they needed, then shop around and buy knockoffs or inferior versions of items I had shown them. Or they would somehow succeed in buying products for a few dollars less from another designer. I wanted to trust my clients. The very idea that someone would pose as a customer only to steal what is essentially my 'intellectual property' is not my definition of trustworthiness.

Here's an example and possible solution to what I'm talking about. A woman came into the showroom one day loaded down with all kinds of materials and pictures. She said to me, "I want to pick your brain."

"Sure," I said, "No problem. Let me get a contract and we can discuss whatever you wish."

"Contract?" she asked.

"Yes," I replied, "A contract that includes my hourly rate for brain picking."

This dialogue clearly took her by surprise. My feeling was and still is - it ain't free baby! Like any other professional I have a degree, many years of experience, and access to an abundance of resources and contacts in the business that I'd painstakingly gathered over many years. So, ask yourself, would you go into a doctor's office, and in good conscience ask the doctor for a consultation that may ultimately cure you, only to walk away without paying? Obviously interior design is not a life-or-death healthcare situation, but I think you get the gist. (See Sample Retainer Contract below.)

INTERIOR DESIGN PLAN
RETAINER CONTRACT

Date: _______________

Client: _______________________________

The Interior Designer will meet with client to define requirements of project.

A retainer fee of $_________ will be a draw against the Interior Design plan as listed:

- Field measure for floor plans
- Space planning
- Design concepts
- Cost estimates
- Delivery, installation, and supervision of product

The hourly rate of $__________ will be recorded, deducted from the retainer fee, and will not exceed the agreed retainer amount.

If client decides to proceed with the project, the retainer fee may be applied to the ending balance. There will be no refunds once the Interior Design Plan is approved, and a 50% deposit is placed. No exceptions.

The sum of $______________ is hereby received.

Client Signature: _______________________________

Interior Designer Signature: _________________________

Here is another vampirism scenario. One Saturday afternoon a client, let's call her Margo, visited the showroom. Margo was new to the area and needed several items for her new home. After discussing generalities of the scope of work and what she wanted to accomplish, she requested an appointment for me to visit her home. Margo was very friendly, and I trusted her because she divulged what her budget was right up front. I agreed to come to her home, measure and create a floor plan, and take pictures. One of her wish-list items was a chandelier which, in her eyes, would be the focal point of the design. After our meeting in her home, we set a follow-up date. I told her I would have some options for her on light fixtures as well as paint colors, area rugs and fabrics.

A few days later she stopped by my office, and I presented the ideas I felt would work best in her home within her budget and the style of her home. Margo seemed to be overjoyed and approved everything I presented including her coveted chandelier. We set yet another appointment for me to come to her home to see how the samples I had pulled would work on site.

When I met Margo at her home, she told me she was eager for me to see a few items she had purchased since our last meeting.

"Okay," I responded enthusiastically and as I walked into her home, lo and behold, there hanging in her dining room was an almost exact, but clearly less expensive copy of the light fixture I had shown her in my office. Naturally she asked my opinion about her new acquisition. Lucky for her I did not express the first thing that came to mind. Instead, I stated that I thought it worked fine.

"But I'm sorry Margo," I added, "I will not go any further with your project until you agree to sign a contract and provide a retainer fee." End of story.

It was not my intention to be a stickler about this, but having been burned in the past; I sincerely believe clients value your interior design expertise when they pay for it. Besides, I had already invested many hours on this project and felt that I had built a relationship based on trust. Fortunately, Margo agreed to my terms. Unfortunately, the light fixture she chose still hangs sadly cheapening my beautiful design to this day.

SNESs

The next type of vampire is the Super-Needy-Energy-Sucking vampire, or SNES. SNESs are established clients that want your complete and undivided attention all the time. Please beware; they are not always only after just design consultation. Some want a designer/life-coach/bestie. Honestly, I didn't mind listening to client's personal life and becoming a quasi-confidante. Sometimes it was quite amusing. However, setting boundaries with these types of clients while presenting a professional image at all times can be a tricky balancing act. I discovered clients wanted to share very personal details about their lives with me. Yup, including their sex lives. I listened warily, but never violated their trust.

To me, my personal life was just that, personal. It got to the point that I had to silence my phone after 7PM otherwise the SNES species vampires would text me, call me, email me, all hours of the day and night, on my days off, during doctor's visits, holidays, birthdays, vacations – you name it. You don't see me showing up to their homes in the wee hours of the night just to show them a new fabric I found for their sectional, do you?

Of course, work is important. But it is also very important to maintain a social life and be able to occasionally take a break from work. Being creative is a wonderful gift, but it's also a gift that can quickly burn you out and be all consuming, which can seriously affect your overall mental and physical health.

I would caution not to get too involved with clients. When you have SNES vampires that want to speak to you 24/7 my recommendation is – do not respond immediately. Creating a little boundary is essential for your well-being. Clients do understand but sometimes feel they can break that boundary. I always tried to respond back as quickly as possible, and I always treated them with appreciation and respect. But there were occasions where I had to push back and explain why I didn't get back as quickly as they may have liked. Most got it. Some didn't.

As an interior designer, I always had multiple projects and many clients to balance simultaneously. It can be a challenge to keep everyone happy, and always meet their sometimes-unreasonable expectations while maintaining a relationship that is both businesslike and amicable. Protecting yourself is of huge importance. Clients need to understand and value your expertise. In any case, all the schooling, training and experience you have earned does not come from nothing. It's also about respect.

By the way, I do *not* bring up fees with clients in the very beginning, unless asked. I was flexible knowing everyone had a proposed budget each with different needs, wants, and resources. Most of my clients were successful professionals and I knew they did not achieve success by giving away information and or knowledge. It was part of my job to make clients understand that my expertise and experience comes with a price. Being gracious about compensation and being very clear is nothing to be embarrassed about. In other words, I had no problem reminding myself that I was not a nonprofit business, and I expected to be compensated for my services. I am not saying I overcharged clients. I am saying there is value in what I did as a professional interior designer. Once the discussion about cost was settled the pressure was released, and we could enjoy the process.

SHOW ME THE SHOWROOM

A bit more about the showroom. I define a showroom as a space where various products are displayed for conceptual ideas and purchase. For example, there were various staged vignettes in the showroom where I worked that displayed bedroom, living room, and dining room furnishings. Light fixtures were suspended throughout the showroom to feature each of the vignettes. Also on display were various pieces of art, mirrors, lamps, as well as a variety of both large and small plants, small to medium sized faux trees, and accessories.

Overall, the showroom was a stunning display of eye-candy to view and take in. In addition, there were racks upon racks of fabrics organized by vendor and color hanging neatly on a wall that spanned the length of the entire building. There were area rugs, wood and carpet flooring samples, tile samples, paint chip samples, wallpaper and more. The showroom was a one-stop shopping resource for clients and designers.

WHAT'S UPS?

I worked with other showroom interior designers that were onsite, and the only fair way to receive new clients was a system we created called, 'ups.' 'Ups' is a systematic rotation in which everyone has an opportunity to meet and greet people when they come into the showroom. So, if it was my 'up,' I would greet the potential client. If my 'up' did not pan out to be a possible client because I didn't set an in-home appointment or sell them an item off the floor, it would be the next designer's attempt at bat – their 'up.'

Writing about 'ups' reminds me about a time when I used to worry about getting new business. I finally stopped worrying once I realized I had no control over who came through the showroom door, or how I would be perceived. But for reasons I will explain, clients were drawn to me. I consider myself a spiritual person, and as such I relied on my spirituality to ask for the 'right clients.' By 'right clients' I do not mean those who appear to have the biggest budget. In fact, several clients who had seemingly unlimited budget were often those who ostensibly had bad attitudes and absolutely no taste whatsoever. Right clients were,

87

instead, those I could work with mutually. My belief was maybe those clients came into my life for reasons beyond just needing my professional interior design assistance. I often felt they were there to teach me something about myself as well. I always took away many lessons from a project, mostly rewarding, but some not so rewarding.

Oh, unrewarding lessons you ask? You want to hear about some of those, don't you? Yes, dealing with impudent clients was unrewarding. In my experience though, the rewards far outweighed the annoyances. But sometimes I had to convince myself I could work with clients with bad behavior, or maybe I could at the very least help them somehow. Since I was always under a lot of pressure to sell, I had to convince myself that a little pain would not hurt me. But as you read on you will discover that I was wrong. I learned I couldn't make everyone happy, that is their walk and their choice. If someone is going to treat you poorly in the beginning of the relationship, it is my experience that they are very unlikely to change. So, I would ask, 'Why put myself in an abusive situation?'

YOU WANT MORE DIRT – YOU GOT IT!

Here's what I'm talking about. I recall greeting a woman in the showroom and we began to chat. I asked her what brought her into the showroom this day.

Without warning she boldly and abruptly announced, "Never-mind that, I always get what I want."

It was as though I should have gotten a memo with this information prior to her arrival. I thought to myself, 'I'll bet this one comes at a price!'

Nevertheless, I listened to her and offered her a tour around the showroom and explained how I worked. I handed her my card and said that I had to leave for an appointment, but feel free to contact me if I could be of assistance.

She said, "Go ahead, leave, I don't give a s#&@!"

Wow, shocking to say the least. Apparently, she must have felt she did not get her way in this instance. I chose not to respond, wished her a good day, and made a mental note that I would probably not be a good fit for her, and vice-versa.

<h3 style="text-align:center">MARY, CAN YOU HEAR ME?</h3>

Another example of, let's say, misbehavior was a client I had been patiently trying to work with for a least a month. I'll call her Mary. When Mary would stop by the showroom I would inwardly groan, knowing I would be spending valuable time with her making zero headway on her project. Honestly, I was beginning to wonder if she really had a project or whether she was actively living out some strange furnishing-fantasy. Or maybe she didn't have the money on hand to pull the trigger and was just playing me to hold a spot for now. At any rate, she just could not make up her mind on anything and consequently could not make the decision to move forward.

On top of that, Mary visited the showroom often. On this day, we went round-and-round as usual looking at fabrics several of which I had pulled and had shown her before. During our reoccurring exercise of looking at fabrics, checking out fabrics, returning fabrics, reviewing and re-hashing fabric after fabric after fabric, Mary found it necessary to constantly chit-chat about everything except – fabric. She was such a motor-mouth I could hardly get a word in edge wise and decided to just let her go off. I thought to myself, '...if she exercised her physique like she does her mouth, she'd be an Olympic Gold-Medalist'. Ironically, Mary eventually felt compelled to remind me that she too has a voice regarding her project and for some reason she felt she was not being heard.

'Excuse me?' Kill me now, I'm begging you.

She should have considered that my apparent sudden hearing loss may have been caused by the din created by the constant irrelevant flapping of her gums. At any rate, I gave her my full attention and listened as I had been listening for weeks on end. Once she got everything off her chest, she started to listen back for a change and together we, at long last, moved forward with her project.

ANNIE AIN'T GONNA' SING THE BLUES

A couple came into the showroom one quiet Saturday afternoon. I greeted them and introduced myself. Sam and Annie explained to me they had just sold their very large home in town and downsized to a condo. They also recently purchased a condo that was being built in the mid-west and were just beginning to shop around for what they wanted.

I walked them through the showroom while they asked me several questions about how we worked. I told them we were very flexible in how we worked because everyone had different needs. I expressed I was interested in what their wishes were for their new home and, as always, stated that it was about them, not me. We had a great conversation, and they were interested in hiring me after listening to my philosophy and how I practiced my craft.

During our tour in the showroom, Annie spied a small piece of art. She claimed she just had to have this little jewel. The original painting was very colorful – oranges and yellows all of which were her favorite colors. Annie said this was to be my inspiration on the colors she wanted in her new home. Strangely though, there was a little blue in the painting and she stated, "But absolutely no blue!" Oh no, was she going to be like No-Go-Green Elizabeth and tell me that blue is not a color either because it's in the sky? Thankfully, that didn't happen. Annie purchased the painting and asked me to keep it for now, so I hung it in my office. This became my first project that was inspired and designed using the colors of a painting – minus the blue of course.

As they were leaving the showroom Annie told me that they decided on me for their project mainly because I stated that this was about them and not me. She further told me she had worked with many interior designers over the years. Sadly, Annie told me those interior designers pretty much made the project all about them.

THE FIREPLACE FIVE

It was a soft grey rainy day in February when I opened the showroom doors. A very tall elderly man neatly dressed in well-pressed Khakis slacks, a long white sleeve button down shirt, a Gucci belt and loafers

91

walked towards me. He said, "Do you talk to old guys?"

I said, "I talk to everyone!"

I introduced myself and he said his name was Jim. He proceeded to tell me that he wasn't sure why he was in the showroom, but oddly enough asked if he could have a personal tour.

While we ambled our way through the showroom, Jim had a lot to say about his 50-year marriage and the three homes he owned. He explained to me that his wife was in a care facility for Alzheimer's and how much he missed her. Jim told me a charming story about when they were building their home. She insisted on having a fireplace in the master bedroom.

"That fireplace ended up costing me a lot of money!" Jim remarked.

I looked at him and wondered what he meant.

"It was because of that fireplace we had five daughters!"

Immediately I was interested in everything Jim had to say, and I knew he was filled with all kinds of great stories.

His daughters now had families of their own, all of them out of state. I could sense Jim was a bit lonely and wanted to talk. He told me he wanted to update the home he maintained as his primary residence but didn't know where to begin. I suggested we start by making an appointment and I would come to his home. I told him I would schedule plenty of time to discuss the possibilities and what he wanted to achieve. This pleased him and it marked the beginning of a very sweet friendship.

I thoroughly enjoyed working with Jim on his home and getting it updated and situated the way he wanted. We had just wrapped things up when Jim had health issues and could no longer live alone, and his home went on the market. He went to live in a beautiful care facility and asked if I would help him spruce things up. I had the pleasure of designing his two-bedroom apartment in his new digs and placing some of the special items from his home into his new abode. Jim always had a positive outlook on life, and I treasure the sweet stories he shared with me. He was always a kind considerate gentleman.

CLAIRE & QUEENIE

Now on to Claire. The first time I met Claire, I noticed her small lean stature and a walk that indicated she was on a mission. Her blonde hair was like spun sprayed cotton candy and was shaped like a helmet on top of her tiny head. No stray hair dares to escape this formation. Her walk and posture stated she did not put up with nonsense from anyone. Claire was very petite and always wore beautifully tailored clothes, often with a bright floral top, and of course stylish designer shoes. Her manicure was always perfect with mauve lacquered nails that were skillfully shaped into small daggers on each of her tiny fingers. I noticed a humongous emerald cut diamond ring on her mildly arthritic ring finger. Claire wore large round diamond earrings that were large enough to peak out from under her helmet of hair. She carried the largest Louis Vuitton bag I have ever seen, and in it lounged a black, well-groomed doggie she called Queenie. When little-tiny Claire made an entrance, she did it big.

Come what may, she picked me to assist her in various small projects for the four homes her family owned. We got along great because she was very direct, she did not mince words. Claire always knew what she wanted, when she wanted it, and how she wanted it. She never did any major projects, although she regularly dangled the carrot that she planned to completely remodel her homes one day. She never did, but she always managed to keep me busy with some project or another.

Claire was constantly on the move, going to and from her homes and traveling the world. She was a perfectionist and took immense pride in her looks and in her homes. I really enjoyed working with her.

The majority of the clientele that visited the showroom in the last years of my practice had success, wealth, worldly experience, and time. All of them lived, and presumably continue to live in several homes in various locations in the U.S. and worldwide. More often than not, my clients knew exactly what they wanted – which sometimes made things easy. However, I discovered many could be set in their own ways, which sometimes made things not-so-easy. For those not-so-easy clients I knew I had to present options, and in a delicate way. I sensed that if I had to push the envelope, it had to be done very gently.

So, there you have it, a few inside dirt stories. Some grimy, some sweet, but all true. After all, you truly cannot make this stuff up.

CHAPTER 12
TEACHING – AN APPLE ON MY DESK

I always thought I would enjoy teaching or mentoring and the opportunity to do so came about not long after the showroom opened. Shannon, a friend of my daughter's, was enrolled in an interior design program and approached me requesting an internship which, with the approval of the showroom's owner, I gladly accepted. Shannon was only available on Saturdays, and as luck would have it that was one of the days I worked. Thankfully, most Saturdays were slow, and, with Shannon's help and the free time gave me a chance to catch up. So, I directed Shannon to a mish-mash collection of various samples and tasked her with sorting and putting them away. Although tedious and clearly not much fun, the task provided Shannon the hands-on experience she needed to learn specific manufacturers.

This was not Shannon's only task. When time allowed, I would show her my projects and explain the design concept and how I arrived at what I was planning. I also gave Shannon an opportunity to pull items so she could learn and experience what it was like to work on a project, how to build on an idea, explore options, possibilities, and especially, how to make a project fun. We also spent time going through the showroom's websites of exclusively held product

95

lines. I like to think that the short amount of time we worked together was a great opportunity for Shannon. It helped support her decision to become an interior designer which she, in fact did and continues to do successfully to this day.

Shannon's tutelage, like any worthwhile endeavor, required hard work and dedication. It is my strong belief that it was important for her to see the humbling behind-the-scenes 'grunt-worthy' side of the business. After all, the interior design business is not always as glamorous as one might think.

ASSISTANCE PLEASE!

Later, as my business grew, I went to our showroom owner and told him I desperately needed help. After all, my job was about selling and there was no way I could be three places at once – on the showroom floor, at a client's home, or in the office designing and selling projects. I was falling behind and I was completely stressing. I knew that if I continued at this frenzied pace the company would suffer from a loss of business, or I would go completely bat-crap crazy trying to juggle my overwhelming workload.

The owner agreed and suggested I find an assistant that both he and I would share. Truth be told, I already had someone in mind that I thought would be a perfect fit. The person I recommended was a young woman named Sophie who had recently contacted me expressing that she was considering a career in the interior design profession. She was also a friend of the family. Sophie went to school with my daughter, and I had known her and her mother for some time.

I contacted recent-college-graduate Sophie and told her she could come in for an interview. Happily, she was hired. The problem though was the only space left in the showroom was my already cramped tiny office. Somehow, we made our cozy little space work and, although Sophie did not report to me directly, she was with me a great deal of the time during the day. It was a wonderful opportunity to give her simple tasks early on and then build from there. She was eager to learn, and I always had something for her to do when she was available.

Sophie became very knowledgeable very quickly on all the manufacturers the showroom regularly depended on, and she was one of the rare design assistants that quickly caught on to my organized chaos work method. Even after we had gotten to know each other better, I often took it for granted that Sophie would instinctively know what I thinking or wanting without me was asking. In hindsight, it was a bit unfair on my part to make this assumption, and I do take the blame for not noticing or commending her valuable innate abilities. My excuse was that I was constantly slammed at work trying to stuff ten pounds into a five-pound bag and pressured to get everything done quickly and on time. With that said though, I credit Sophie with making me a better communicator and curbing my tendency to be impatient. I never said or thought my design assistants should be able to walk on water, or read my mind, but sometimes they had other very useful superpowers!

It was such a great thing for me to be able to teach and share my ideas and experience with Sophie. I truly wanted to set her up for success, show her how I worked, and offer her guidance that allowed her to make her own decisions and artistically express herself in a way best for her.

CHAPTER 13
BALANCE – TRYING TO WALK A TIGHTROPE BACKWARDS

To get through this final chapter, I'm going to ask you to join me and go back in time. After a 30-year marriage, I got divorced. For a long time after my divorce, I felt completely isolated and as though I was trapped underwater. I was ashamed and embarrassed. I had always been successful and very competitive, yet I felt I had failed at my marriage, and to me a failed marriage meant I lost. This was one of the most difficult times of my life.

To get out of my stay-at-home mom mode I decided to go to real estate school with the hope I'd resurface and climb out of my hole. I earned my license and started working in commercial real estate. But I was still unhappy, and I knew I had to make changes to both my career and my life. Anxiety and fear were my daily companions. I had a lot on my plate and there were many questions I had to answer and paths I had to navigate. I had to resolve all the 'what's?' in my life. What was going to make me happy? What do I really want? What do I do next? These questions and more kept resurfacing and muddling up my thinking. My biggest challenge at hand was I had to fight off my biggest monster – fear.

So, after about a year in real estate – which I hated by the way – I boldly ignored the fear monster, resigned my real estate position, and decided to move back 'home' to Southern California to regroup and figure things out. Fortunately, my two children were grown by this time, one almost out of college, the other just starting college. Nevertheless, I was anxious about leaving the state, my friends, my children, and the comfortable life I was blessed to enjoy for so many years. My daughter encouraged my decision to return to So Cal. "Just give it a try mom," she said.

I felt I owed myself this chance to collect my thoughts and focus on easing my uncertainty about the future.

I had several interviews lined up in Los Angeles, but I wasn't thrilled with my prospects after meeting with the various companies. It didn't take long before I knew in my gut my move back to Southern California was not working. It did give me pause to think about how I could move forward though, and I felt more empowered by my bold move and, I'll say, short California adventure before diving into the next chapter. Although I have family and friends in So Cal, and the sunny beachside cities will always have a special place in my heart, it just didn't feel like home to me anymore. I had to move on.

SORRY TO EAT & RUN, BUT
I'M GOING TO BE A ROCK STAR!

So while biding my time in So Cal, I investigated jobs back in Arizona and found several that sounded promising. As luck would have it, an acquaintance told me about a position being offered with a friend I had worked with in the furniture business while doing part time free-lance work. He was planning to open a new showroom and needed an interior designer. I reached out and decided if there is no risk, there is no opportunity. I was offered the position.

Still in So Cal, it was Thanksgiving Day and one of my sisters was hosting a wonderful turkey dinner. We were standing around the kitchen counter when my sisters asked, "How's the job search going?"

"It's great!" I said, "I got a job back in Arizona."

So, I didn't actually move on – I moved back instead. Be that as it may, I was excited to move back to Arizona. I knew I would immediately feel at home and happy to be back in my new/old town and fortunate to have new prospects. The new job was a big break for me, and a chance to hit the refresh button. I was given the go-ahead to restart my career in the field I truly loved and an opportunity to grow and begin a new life. Excited for the challenge and all this positive new direction – the fear monster eventually shriveled up and withered away.

Shortly after Thanksgiving I prepared to head back to Arizona. Like a boss, I rented a truck and trailer to haul all my belongings and car. The timing was perfect as the showroom wasn't due to open until after the holiday season. In the meantime, there was much to do and learn. I studied the product lines the showroom offered for days. I also realized I would have to make sure my wardrobe was killer. My goal was to be a rock star interior designer, and this was my chance.

The showroom did extremely well right from the start. I worked my tail off to acquire clients and projects. The showroom offered many styles of furnishings and services. It was exciting for me to be back in the saddle and running full speed ahead. And I do mean run, literally. Running all over the showroom, running to greet clients, running to visit client's homes, running to prepare proposals, going to trade only showrooms, preparing floor plans, estimates, meeting new vendors, salespeople and designing. Whew! The work was extremely demanding, plus I didn't have help in the beginning. I was simultaneously learning new product lines, assisting in setting up the new showroom, planning and executing projects, getting new business, and working with clients.

WORKITTY-WORK-WORK-WORK!

It took working between 50 and 60 hours a week to really launch my own business within the showroom's business. I did not have the time or energy to socialize or make new friends. I totally and completely immersed myself in my work putting aside old friends, possible new friends, and sadly, my family as well. The only justification for my break-neck pace, the only driving factor was – you guessed it – money.

The F word was out of my life. Not that F word! I'm talking about Fun. My personal life was indeed utterly boring, but at least I had great clothes and shoes! Some consolation, right? Well, fortunately, I loved going to work and meeting new clients in my great new clothes and great new shoes. My thoughts and goals were simple – be very successful. For me that was all encompassing and required 110% of my attention.

Naturally I was fried at the end of each work week, and my clients – bless their silly hearts – were in constant contact with me. I often found myself in the role of part time therapist to clients in addition to everything else I was handling. Clients felt they were free to tell me about everything from what happened in the kitchen, to what did or did not happen in the bedroom – TMI I would argue. Indeed, I was an active listener, but I didn't share much about myself mainly because there was not much to tell. Looking back, I suppose my clicnt's openness was a positive thing. Apparently, they felt comfortable enough to trust me with their secrets, and they must have felt that the things they told me would go no further – which they never did.

It took me about three years to build my business to where I wanted it, and I was thrilled. My success allowed me to go where I wanted and do what I wanted. Finally, I thought I was in a comfortable place to let up on the gas pedal just a little. But I didn't.

THE DOCTOR WILL BE RIGHT IN TO SEE YOU – NOT!

One day while installing a project I noticed I was feeling out of sorts. But I pressed on because my clients were out of town and, as usual, I promised them all would be complete when they returned. Throughout the day though, I grew anxious as I was really feeling unwell, and things were not going as quickly as I wanted. I was distracted with how awful I felt, but I did not want to delay the install. When my team and I were finally finished and headed back to my office, I began to feel even worse. I assumed I probably just had a touch of the flu. My client project list was maxed out, so the timing for a bout of flu could not have been worse.

I decided to go to see my doctor with the hopes of a quick fix. After checking in at the doctor's office I met with the nurse who routinely took my blood pressure. She seemed puzzled by the reading though, so she took it a second time. The nurse seemed disturbed by the second blood pressure reading as well. She had a concerned look on her face when she told me, "Just relax, the doctor will be with you in just a moment," and quickly stepped out of the room.

Next thing I knew, five very large EMT firemen entered the already cramped patient care room and began examining me. They gave me aspirin and being my usual stubborn self, I told them I didn't like taking aspirin. They just smiled and told me again politely, you must take the aspirin, and informed me they were going to take me to the hospital. I naively asked, "What?" and told them, "No, that's okay; you don't have to do that. I drove myself here so I can drive myself to the hospital." I then asked, "Why are you telling me I need to go to the hospital anyway?"

Their response – "Because you're having a heart attack."

What?! A heart attack? I was dumfounded! "This can't be happening," I told myself. I'm in shape, I work out, I eat healthy foods. I have things to do, places to go, people to see. What gives here? But more than that I sensed that a heart attack, although a hard pill to swallow, was the wakeup call I somehow anticipated and perhaps, badly needed.

Who in their right-mind 'needs' a heart attack you ask? Let me explain. My heart attack forced me to take time to recover and during my recovery I came to the realization that this life we are given is not a rehearsal. Nope, not even a dress-rehearsal. Its show time folks and we are live! How easy it was for me to forget all the gifts I had been given and be so completely consumed by a job.

My point in telling this part of my story is that feeling stressed all of the time eventually catches up with a person, even those who think they are superheroes. Sorry to say that even though I truly believed I was a superhero, I was not, and this realization presented me with a huge problem. I knew I would have to figure out a solution that would ensure my self-preservation, while at the same time not jeopardize the strides I had made in my business. I had to somehow find balance and create boundaries. I had to learn how to walk my tightrope backwards.

My heart attack taught me that there is no job that is worth or more important than my health and wellbeing. Yeah sure, I could make a six-figure plus salary, but it won't do me any good if I'm too ill to enjoy the rewards of all my hard work. And apparently you can't take your salary with you when you're gone. So, with that said, being happy in whatever you choose to do in life should be a top priority, and no one is happy when they are sick. Albeit a cliché – don't do it just for the money. I consider myself living proof that if you're good at what you love, the money really will come. Happiness is contagious, and when you're happy, good things will come your way.

We have all had our ups and downs, me included. But through it all I kept my sense of humor and continue to be grateful for many things in my life. I truly believe that being grateful is essential in everyday life. For me, being grateful gave me the strength to embark on a new journey to restart my life after my divorce. I don't know how others find and cultivate gratitude, but I started out with the most important thing – gratitude for my children. Then I worked my way toward gratitude for my career, then, gratitude for my home, and so on. I kept investing in my gratitude bank (and still do) and life seemed to open its arms up to me. With gratitude, it became easier for me to find joy, peace, and the positive side to just about everything and everyone.

Maybe my heart attack was a blessing in disguise in that it forced me to take a large step back and analyze myself, and my life. Albeit a tough way to learn a lesson, and one I certainly do not recommend. But I realized I don't always have to be so hard on myself and constantly run around, hair-on-fire, pedal to the metal, 24/7/365.

I had to ask myself, 'Why do I need to be exhausted all of the time, intolerant and generally indifferent towards everyone and everything?' The answer: no need at all. So, after recovery I applied the heart attack lessons I had learned. I learned to cool my jets, have a deeper appreciation for my family and friends, and be grateful for my home and the wonderful clients and business I successfully built.

The result – I continued to have career success, earned the six-figure plus salary, made incredible friends, met the man of my dreams, and happily remarried. I am now retired and each day I continue to invest in my gratitude bank.

About the Author

Julie Regan Smith enjoys spending time with family and friends, cooking, researching, and trying out new recipes, maintaining an herb garden, exercise, and travel. Julie and her husband happily reside in Southwestern United States.

Email address: greenisnotacolor2023@gmail.com